To Houston.

After all these years

Here's a book!

[signature]

**Iain Hector Ross** grew up in Glasgow in the leafy West End enclave of Kelvingrove. Having a father from Skye and a mother from Lewis meant Gaelic was not only the language of the home but also of the endless procession of cousins and characters who came to *ceilidh*. Together with epic summer journeys 'home' to the islands, these gatherings fed his love of Highland lore, and he has been crafting stories from this source ever since as: feature writer, documentary producer, playwright, singer songwriter and broadcaster. Musically he has performed in English and Gaelic as a soloist and with his group *Trosg* and with *Coisir Gaidhlig Inbhir Nis* (Inverness Gaelic Choir) at Celtic Connections, Belladrum Festival and the Market Bar in Inverness. His radio play *The Coffin Road* was broadcast on BBC radio. While writing *The Whisky Dictionary* he was also helping to create the first legal distillery on the Isle of Raasay. Iain Hector Ross lives in Inverness with his wife, Marion, and two grown-up daughters' occasional bedrooms.

**Ben Averis** is a professional artist and botanist. Originally from Wales, he graduated in Fine Art from Bath Academy of Art in 1980. He combines his art and botanical work through shared subject matter and shared processes, and has illustrated a number of books including *The Rainforests of Britain and Ireland* by Clifton Bain, published by Sandstone Press in 2015. He lives in East Lothian with his wife Alison and daughter Elen. His artwork can be seen on his website: www.benaverisart.co.uk

# THE
# WHISKY
# DICTIONARY

Iain Hector Ross

Illustrated by Ben Averis

SANDSTONEPRESS
HIGHLAND | SCOTLAND

Published in Great Britain by
Sandstone Press Ltd
Dochcarty Road
Dingwall
Ross-shire
IV15 9UG
Scotland.

www.sandstonepress.com

The publisher acknowledges support from Creative Scotland
towards publication of this volume.

ISBN: 978-1-910985-92-2
ISBNe: 978-1-910985-93-9

Cover illustrations by Ben Averis
Cover design by Raspberry Creative Type
Typeset by Iolaire Typesetting, Newtonmore
Printed and bound by CPI Group (UK) Ltd, Croydon, CR0 4YY

# CONTENTS

*Do Mòr, Cairistiona agus Susanna*
*This book is dedicated to Marion, Christina and Susanna*

# INTRODUCTION

This Whisky Dictionary is the first guide to the language written from within the industry. From the floor of the still house to the malt barn's pagoda roof, it gathers the keywords and delves deep into its production process and colourful history. The recent wave of renewed worldwide interest means we live in an era when folk of all nationalities and cultures can meet and find themselves talking the 'language of whisky'. Sharing and savouring their passion for the Universal Dram, they use the rich language that has evolved around this ancient and complex spirit.

Informative, entertaining and passionate, the Whisky Dictionary is a unique guide to the special vocabulary shared by whisky makers and whisky lovers the world over. So, pop the cork and release the unique aromas and flavours of the language. Close your eyes, breathe in the vapour and be taken straight to the ageing oak cask and the dank warehouse where the spirit lies maturing for so many years.

Like no other manufactured product, Scotch whisky is on a centuries-long journey of engagement with all peoples and cultures. The evidence of its arrival in new regions is reflected in the growth in overseas visitors coming to Scotland in search of the distilleries and the people who make the whisky they love. Their cheerful passion can make some of us Scots seem almost blasé about our gift to the world. Scotch whisky tourism has become a serious part of the industry and an important income stream. In addition, at time of writing, thirty new distillery projects are being built across the country, a construction boom not seen for at least a generation.

Every corner of the landscape has its own whisky story, and Scotland has been inventing and reinventing ways to produce this spirit for centuries; from fiery, one day old, illicit mountain whisky to velvety 40 year old, single malt, sherry cask finished, masterpieces secured deep in the spirit vaults at the heart of the capital city of Edinburgh. Records show we've been talking, reading, writing and even arguing about the stuff since at least the 16th century and, as the art of production has evolved and changed, so has its language. The history of whisky is one of invention, crafting, refining and reinvention through periods of boom and bust, prohibition and legislation, smuggling and skirmishes, and vast international outreach.

The story is also one of a simple crafted spirit called Scotch whisky that has connected with people from the Wild West to the Far East, from the Frozen North to the Beautiful South, to become a recognised token of fellowship. It is the acknowledged drink for those special moments when people renew friendships, commemorate moments and celebrate achievements that might include reaching the summit of a mountain, completing eighteen holes in a hailstorm or just putting the kids to bed at the end of a long day. The pouring of the warming dram is the signal to all in the company that it is time to put away concerns and turn to each other and enjoy the *craic*. It fuels our stories and our songs and each bottle carries its own unique sense of place, people and heritage.

Now open your eyes, swill the spirit in the glass and observe how the balanced combination of time, malted barley, oak cask and passionate husbandry takes form in its oily amber golden hues. Sip softly and savour the full depth, intensity and complexity of malted barley, spring water, copper and oak. Add a bead of water and the lighter organic, citrus and vanilla flavours spring open. Then: a final nod to the lovingly poured spirit with the traditional salute and a drop of ancient Gaelic, *Slainte Mhath!* before offing the dram.

**Iain Hector Ross**
Inverness 2017

# THE WHISKY DICTIONARY

Alcohol
CO2
YEAST
Sugar-rich Wort
YEAST FEAST 1 mile
WELCOME TO THE WASHBACKS
Ben Averis 2014

# A

**Abscisic acid** *n.* A concentrate within mature barley grains which acts as an inhibitor to germination. The steeping/soaking process reduces the concentration of abscisic acid (ABA) as the grains begin to germinate. The grain opens as water penetrates the barley and the ABA leeches through the husk. Full germination of the barley grain occurs once the steeping process has reduced the level of ABA in the grain to a relatively low level.

**ABV** *n.* Any liquor's alcoholic strength is measured by its percentage of 'alcohol content by volume', abbreviated as its ABV%. Newly distilled 'new-make' spirit poured from the spirit still is generally around 70% ABV before being diluted with water and filled into the cask at 63.5% ABV for its three years of maturation to become Scotch whisky. At bottling, further dilution generally brings this down to between 40% and 50% ABV. This compares with port/sherry from 15%-20% ABV, wine 7%-14% ABV and beer/cider ranging between 3%-8% ABV.

**Acetaldehyde** *n.* Once the new-make spirit is filled into the cask, oxidation occurs causing chemical reactions in the lignin elements in the wood. These produce successive compound interactions that shape the maturing distilled spirit's flavour. One such reaction is the creation of acetaldehydes and acetic acid from ethanol. These compounds are the flavour congeners that contribute sweeter, fruity tones to the spirits, as opposed to aldehyde compounds which lay down sourer, more bitter notes.

## Acidity

**Acidity** *n*. The natural acidity of whisky at 40% bottling strength is PH 4-4.5. This mildly acidic state is mainly due to the presence of organic acetic acid and other trace acids.

**Ackavity** *n*. (Scots) Archaic traditional Scots name for whisky, derived from dialect pronunciation of 'Aqua vitae', historically used to describe any generic distilled whisky of any strength and quality.

**Active carbon** *n*. The 'active carbon' layer is an important feature in neutralising new-make spirit character and reducing sulphur concentrates. In cask preparation the charring or flaming of the inner wood surface breaks open the surface of the wood's membrane. The direct application of scorching heat also serves to temper the bitterness and astringency in the surface membrane without ultimately contributing to the whisky's eventual colour or flavour. This charred layer now becomes the active carbon threshold between the wood and the spirit, allowing the oak membrane to absorb the spirit. The three-year process of maturation towards whisky continues as the spirit soaks deeper.

**Additional Cask Evolution** *n*. Additional Cask Evolution (ACE) is the creative use by the distiller of specifically chosen casks with distinctive flavour characteristics, for second and third fill finishing. The ACE stage in the finishing of a whisky enables distinctive finishing tones and unusual or unexpected colours to be brought to the whisky. Each distillery tends to have its own special trademark in-house speciality ACE recipe finish. Macallan for example is well known for its custom of transferring its whisky from first use Bourbon barrels for finishing in Spanish sherry casks. ACE enables a spectacular range of colours to be produced, from the pale lemony pallor from virgin oak to the rose blush highlight from Tuscan red wine casks.

**Adenosine triphosphate** *n*. After DNA, adenosine triphosphate (ATP) is the second most important molecule for all animal and plant life as the store for energy from food or sunlight. In distilling, ATP plays a vital role in powering yeast cell growth during fermentation of the wort liquor. This growth is fuelled by sugars stored in the wort creating ATP in the yeast for its own cell growth. Fermentation also creates by-products of alcohol and carbon dioxide ($CO_2$) of no use to the growing organism. The yeast continues to extract energy for its growth until all sugars are exhausted and fermentation naturally dies off. This converts the wort to an alcoholic wash/beer of between 7-11% ABV. The $CO_2$ by-product produced is usually vented directly from the **washbacks** to the open air outside the wash chamber. Some larger capacity distilleries will collect the gas for commercial recycling.

**Aeration** *n*. The venting of air through the wash and spirit as they enter the stills. This activates the liquors, rendering them more reactive to the copper surfaces of the still system. Copper interaction encourages production of soluble copper elements in the spirit. These act on and remove unpleasant sulphur and cyanide compounds. One downside to aerating liquors in the still is that their enhanced 'dynamism' also increases the rate of corrosion of the copper surface elements of the still and reduces the working life of parts of the system. Replacement of these elements can be required after just fifteen years of constant use.

**Aerobic respiration** *n*. Occurs inside all living plant and animal cells where glucose and oxygen interact. Aerobic respiration releases energy in the form of adenosine triphosphate for actions whilst producing carbon dioxide ($CO_2$) and water as by-products. In distilling whisky, the exclusion of oxygen in the sealed washback chambers ensures that anaerobic fermentation takes place, producing ethanol or alcohol as a by-product together with $CO_2$.

**Aftershots**

**Aftershots** *n*. Less commonly used name for the last fraction of the spirit run. More generally referred to as the '**feints**', this is the last and weakest fraction of the spirit to be drawn from the distillation after the '**foreshots**' and the '**heart**'.

**Age Statement** *n*. When whisky is bottled, its age statement reflects the time it has spent maturing in the cask, rounded up to a 'year' number. This indicates the year in which the whisky was transferred from cask to bottle. It has come to be regarded as a key indicator of likely quality and age statements on single malt labels currently tend to be used for whiskies matured for a minimum of 8 years. Age statements are also used in blended whisky for 'deluxe' brands created from many different premium whiskies of different ages and from different casks 'becoming married' together in vatting vessels. For these blends, the Scotch Whisky Regulations require an age statement on the label and packaging. This must reflect the age of the youngest whisky in the blend. For example, a Scotch whisky blending 8, 12, and 15 year old whiskies must carry an age statement that states the blend is '8 years old'.

**Aicher** *n*. (Scots, **ake'er**) A traditional agricultural name for a single ear of barley.

**Air** *n*. Average air temperature and humidity play an important role in the maturation of whisky. There are an estimated 20 million casks of whisky stored maturing in bonded warehouses across Scotland at any one time. The ambient temperature, airflow and air quality in and around these buildings reflects the local climate and contributes to the '**terroir**' influence on the finished whisky. These air factors also govern the evaporation rate or '**Angels' Share**' of the spirit lost to the atmosphere. In cool drier heights of the Highlands and Strathspey and on the Atlantic wind-chilled island coasts evaporation of spirit from each cask is reckoned to be between 0.5-1% lost each year. However, in the warmer, more temperate parts of the world such as the humid climate of **Tasmania** the loss to the atmosphere can range as high as 5-6% of the contents per annum.

**Akvavit** (Norwegian, **Akkevit**) *n.* Straw-coloured Scandinavian spirit, distilled from grain or potatoes. The best akvavit, like Scotch whisky, is finished in oak sherry casks and may be coloured with caramel or amber before bottling at around 45% ABV. In its clear 'taffel' form akvavit is finished by flavouring and colouring from a range of pungent aromatic herbs and spices such as anise, cardamom, cumin and citrus fruit peel. However, whilst Scotch malt whisky lies maturing for years in cool, dark bonded warehouses, the Scandinavian spirit follows its Viking instincts and takes to the sea. Premium Norwegian 'Linje' Akvavit sets off on a voyage of maturity spending four months ploughing the oceans and crossing the equator twice. This unique finishing at sea exposes the spirit to constant agitation in the casks and extreme temperature and humidity changes. All this produces the distinctive Akvavit 'Linje' or 'Line' finish.

**Alabust-beer** *n.* (Scots, **ala'boost**) A colloquial name for any beer agreed to be of superior or exceptional quality.

**Alanine** *n.* Alanine is one of the most slowly absorbed amino acids in the fermentation stage of the wort liquor. It is synthesised and absorbed by the yeast as it grows and reaches next generation bud stage.

**Alchemist** *n.* The ancient ancestor of the modern distiller whose early efforts, experimentation and optimism we should applaud. Across the ages and continents their accumulated common knowledge of plants, herbs, lotions and perfumes developed into the ability to capture their essence in metallic **alembics**, eventually creating potent variations of **aqua vitae** spirit. Originally created for purely altruistic medicinal and invigorating purposes, the recreational benefits of these spirits were soon identified. This encouraged less altruistic alchemists to specialise in the science and process, throwing their energies and resources into the evolving craft of aqua vitae distillation.

**Alchemy** *n.* The traditional pseudo-medicinal science of footering about with lotions, potions, earth, fire, water and base metals. Experimentation with elements to discover formulae for creating long dreamt of but as yet unachievable results *(e.g. the elixir of life, turning lead into gold, and Scotland qualifying for the next World Cup)*. Happily, this ancient vein of scientific endeavour also produced the secret of alembic distillation and, through evolution of the process, led to whisky.

**Alcohol** *n.* (Arabic) Derived from the original Arabic word *Al-Kuhl,* it was first used to describe craft- produced cosmetic and antiseptic powders. Among the earliest detailed references to it as a beverage are those attributed to the Majorcan polymath Ramon Lull (1236-1315) who pronounced; *'The taste of it exceedeth all other tastes, and the smell of it all other smells'* and *'is of marvellous use and commodity a little before the joining in battle to encourage the soldiers' minds.'* The scientific definition of what exactly alcohol is came about in relatively modern times. In Geneva in 1892 alcohol was given the chemical definition name of **Ethanol,** following discussions at the International Conference on Chemical Nomenclature. In the whisky-making process, ethanol makes its first appearance as a by-product of the fermentation of the liquid wort sugars. As the yeast feeds on the sugars in the sealed washback vessels it rapidly grows and produces ethanol and vast quantities of $CO_2$ (Carbon Dioxide) gas. This is a volatile environment and the $CO_2$ must be safely vented to the open air if it cannot be commercially collected. Once the yeast has exhausted all the sugars in the wort it dies off. The alcoholic liquor in the washback is now called '**wash**', a simple citrus flavoured beer with an ABV content of 7-11%.

**Alcohol by Volume** – see **ABV**

**Aldehyde** *n*. One of the key flavour congeners produced during the fermentation as yeast feeds on the wort sugars, transforming the liquor into an alcoholic wash. Aldehydes occur within the group of fusel alcohols occurring as by-products of the fermentation process. These combine with the ethanol to influence the developing flavour. Aldehydes contribute distinctive sour, leafy and unripe notes to the finished whisky taste.

**Ale** *n*. Pot, or burnt, ale is the residue left in base of the wash still after the first batch distillation. It consists of a combination of yeast, proteins, carbohydrates and some trace elements from the copper of the still. Island or coastal distilleries can dispose of pot ales as a bio waste product via long pipelines to the sea, if local geography and ecology permits. Inland distilleries collect and store the ale for further processing. Traditionally it is used to make pot ale syrup for pig and cattle feed. It is also dried by evaporation to mix with **draff** to produce animal feed pellets known as 'Barley Dark Grains'.

**Alembic** *n*. Generic name for the simple vessel forming the oldest and most basic apparatus and method for distilling quantities of spirit. Universally, the alembic design comprises an onion-shaped copper chamber for heating the liquid tapering to a long, narrow neck and cap at the top. This shape feeds the rising hot vapour up and out via a copper pipe. The pipe outfall is sunk into a cold-water tub where the vapour condenses to be collected as the distilled liquor.

**Amalgamation** *n*. A form of business merger or consolidation which occurs frequently and regularly throughout the history of the whisky industry. Amalgamation has been a constant from the establishment of small-scale local stills in the 18th century to the huge industrial grain distillers of the 20th century and the dominant multinational spirit giants of the present. Countless independent

**American barrel**

whisky distillers have grown, established their brand and found a market, only to founder as unforeseen changes forced them to give up their identity and independence. Throughout, the industry has survived on this continuous carrying stream of mergers and amalgamations. For some this has been of mutual benefit, most famously in the 19th century when many of Scotland's most successful distilleries amalgamated in 1877 to begin the 100-year global reign of the giant Distillers Company.

**American barrel** *n.* This standard sized 195 litre barrel is the most commonly used cask for storing and maturing Scotch whisky. The sourcing and supply of these barrels in shipments from the United States is informally guaranteed to Scotland's whisky industry by way of the requirements of the U.S. Bourbon Whisky Federal Standards of Identity regulations. These rules specify that Bourbon whisky must be 'stored at not more than 125° proof in charred new oak containers; and also includes mixtures of such whiskies of the same type.' This requirement hugely benefits Scotch whisky producers by ensuring a guaranteed, continuous supply of spirit-ready, charred casks perfect for filling with new-make whisky.

**American Whiskey** *n.* Now experiencing something of a revival after decades of stagnation, the American whiskey industry is enjoying an uplift in the growth of the craft distillery sector and specialist expressions of the traditional major brands. According to the *U.S. Standards of Identity*, American 'whiskey' is divided into six categories: Bourbon, Rye, Rye Malt, Corn, Wheat and Malt whisky. Despite the adopted customary American spelling of 'whiskey', the U.S. legislation is spelled out using the original Scottish spelling of 'whisky'. Other than Corn whisky, all must be produced: 'not exceeding 160° proof from a fermented mash of not less than 51 percent corn, rye, wheat, malted barley, or malted rye grain, respectively, and stored at not more than 125° proof in charred new oak containers'. Corn whisky on the other hand is produced, 'not exceeding 160° proof from a fermented mash of not less than 80 percent corn grain, and if stored in oak containers stored at not more than 125° proof in used or uncharred new oak containers and not subjected in any manner to treatment with charred wood; and also includes mixtures of such whisky.' The industry has its roots in waves of immigration from Scotland and Ireland in the 19th and early 20th centuries. With these immigrants came the skills and business awareness to distil and market the spirit. The ready and increasing availability of competitively priced corn/maize ensured production was possible on a large scale. As the population expanded across the continent so demand for the spirit grew and the building of 'whiskey' distilleries became an attractive long-term investment.

**Amino acids** n. Each protein molecule of all living organisms consists of a combination of hundreds of thousands of amino acid molecules. These fundamental organic compounds are also present in the grains and cereals used in distilling. The introduction of water during malting, known as hydrolysis or steeping, together with increasing temperature, triggers actions in the chains of amino acids which become visible through germination of roots and shoots. In the fermentation stage, amino acid actions result in the production of **ethanol**.

**Amylase** n. The all-important enzyme triggering the breaking down of starch into fermentable sugars. Amylase is uniquely familiar to all of us because it is present in our own saliva. Its abilities and effect can easily be distinguished and tasted in the mouth in the noticeable 'sweetening' experienced when we chew high starch, low sugar, foods such as rice and potatoes. In the Peruvian rainforest, there is an ancient tradition of producing 'masato' liquor by chewing yucca root then storing the mash in jars to ferment into an alcoholic brew. Indeed, all continents have some version of a saliva-mashed, fermentation of rude alcohol liquors. Historically, some brewers even began their fermentations by this reassuringly primitive method of personally chewing the grains to break them down and trigger the amylase. In whisky distilling, amylase does its work in the **mashtuns** when the malted barley grist is mashed at temperatures ranging between 63°C and 95°C. These conditions trigger and sustain amylolysis, converting starch into fermentable sugar, creating the rich sugary wort for the next stage in the process.

**Amylograph** *n.* A device used to measure the level of viscosity, density, or plain porridginess of the slurry produced when cereals are mashed in hot water. An important production measurement which indicates the effective breakdown rate of crystalline starch molecules through gelatinisation in the mash.

**Amylopectin** *n.* The sticky component or polysaccharide that makes up between 70-80% of starch molecules. When broken down by the enzyme **amylase** in the mashing process it produces the distinctive gelatinisation or porridginess of the mash wort liquid. It is also a familiar feature of cookery in the family kitchen where it is commonly seen in the texture of thick risottos, sticky rice and, of course, porridge.

**Amylose** *n.* The non-gelatinising, non-swelling component that comprises around 20-30% of the starch molecule. Although it does not form any gel or paste, it is the simpler starch compound and much more soluble in water than amylopectin.

**Anaerobic digestion** *n.* The breakdown of organic material by bacteria in the absence of oxygen. In whisky distilling this takes place in the washback vessels when yeast feeds on the sugars in the wort and grows until it has exhausted its 'food source'. In these anaerobic conditions this process creates alcohol in the liquor and carbon dioxide ($CO_2$) gas as by-products until all sugar is exhausted and the yeast dies off. This fermentation transforms the sugary wort into an alcoholic citrus-flavoured beer of around 7-11% ABV.

**Analyser** *n.* The primary of the two key column components of the **Coffey or Patent Still** used in the continuous distilling process in large grain distilleries. The analyser column channels the wash through steam heated chambers before it is distilled into spirit in the secondary column, known as the Rectifier. This continuous distilling process, as opposed to the single batch pot still method, was invented by Kilbagie Distillery owner Robert Stein in 1826. His rudimentary but effective design was developed, improved and patented by the Irish distiller Aeneas Coffey. Ironically, though not popular with Irish distillers, the new Coffey system was enthusiastically adopted by the Scottish grain whisky distillers due to its consistency and fast, continuous production. This method of production is also cheaper and simpler in comparison with the pot still distillation method. Today it is used for the bulk of Scotch grain whisky so that 60% of all the whisky in Scotland comes from this continuous distillery production method.

**Angels' share** *n.* The fanciful name for the heady vapour which hangs inside whisky warehouses as the spirit matures and breathes out through the casks. As the maturing whisky interacts with the oak wood the vapour within the cask naturally escapes out through the wood pores into the cool air of the bonded warehouse. In island distilleries, such as Islay, Jura, Mull, Arran, Skye, Harris and Raasay, where warehouses are near the sea, the maturing whisky will take on a hint of the sea air via the porous wood. Depending on mean air temperature, pressure and humidity, between 0.5-2% of the contents can be lost annually to simple evaporation from each of the 20 million casks maturing in Scotland. Sadly, for the distillery workers in the fill store, it is estimated that each barrel they lovingly fill with single new-make spirit will probably lose as much as 6% of its contents over three years into the atmosphere, just waiting to legally become Scotch whisky. Calculating that the average cask is filled with 200 litres to begin with then 1% of around 4 billion litres of whisky is constantly wafting heavenward into the skies above Scotland. But spare a thought for the hard-working distillers in the warm humidity of **Tasmania** where the vapour loss can be as high as 5-6% per annum!

*The Angels' Share* is also the name of award-winning director Ken Loach's 2012 movie which won the Jury Prize at the 2012 Cannes Film Festival. The Scottish comedy drama was filmed at many key whisky locations around Scotland including the Deanston Distillery near Stirling.

**Angels' share fungus** *n*. The popular name for the black colouration found commonly on the timber walls of bonded warehouses. The fungus, *Baudoinia compniacensis*, flourishes on and around any timber and woodland at distillery locations. It thrives on the escaping ethanol vapour, or *'Angels' share'*, which evaporates through the filled oak casks. Its distinctive dark colour is respon-sible for the phenomenon of **warehouse staining**. The fungus was first identified in brandy warehouses in the Cognac region of France. Here it was noticed that over time, the grain and colour of the timber walls was becoming lost under a matt black layer of fungus. A robust organism, the Angels' Share fungus thrives even in Scotland's coldest and bleakest distillery locations where ranks of brooding black hulks create an otherworldly presence in the bare highland landscape.

**Animal feed** *n*. Perhaps partly as a direct continuation of the illicit still smugglers' mantra of *'leave no trace'*, whisky producers have always sought to find a secondary use for all residues and by-products. So it is that a side industry producing animal feed products has grown around whisky production: recycling, reforming and distributing residues from distilling. The primary product in terms of volume is cattle feed in the form of **draff** from the mashing stage comprising the **husks** and solid matter from the mashed **grist**. This has long been recognised and used as a nutritious sugary animal feed. Draff is collected by being cleared from the mashtun through drain holes by the rotating **Lauter blades**. Then it is pumped at high pressure into a draff receiver either for processing on site or removal in wagons for processing elsewhere into wet, dried or pelleted form.

Other feed products from both malt and grain distilling are Pot Ale Syrup, Malt Distillers Dark Grains with Solubles (DDGS), Grain DDGS, Grain moist feeds, and Grain wash syrup. It is estimated that around 60% of distillery by-products are used as feed for cattle, pigs, sheep and horses in Scotland with 40% exported, mainly to the north of England. Historically many distilleries, even in the heart of Glasgow, kept their own well-fed pigs and herds of cattle on site, specifically as a means of recycling distillery waste products. Interestingly, sheep can't be fed any products from a copper pot still as they are particularly sensitive to copper. Strangest husbandry prize must go to Tomatin distillery which until recently sustained its own eel farm.

**Anker** *n*. The smallest sized cask or barrel, usually locally made and commonly used in the 19th century. Although limited with a capacity of around '20 Scotch pints', or 35 litres of spirit, it was ideally suited to the times, being easily handled and hidden and transported on horseback when necessary.

**Antiquary, The** *n*. One of the most iconic and longest lasting blends, still being produced and exported across the world today. Created by John and William Hardie in 1888, it was named after the historical novel by Sir Walter Scott who happened to be their near neighbour and social acquaintance in Edinburgh's New Town. The Antiquary brand today continues under the ownership of Tomatin Distillers and the famous diamond-shaped bottle now offers a choice of three malt blend expressions including a 12 year old and 21 year old.

**Apothecary**

**Apothecary** *n.* The job title of the original prescription chemists who combined their knowledge of medicinal properties of natural plants, herbs, lotions and perfumes with the craft of alembic distilling. These early pharmacists created and dispensed their aromatic aqua vitae spirits of roots and grains as craft medicines for restoring ailing minds and bodies.

**Aqua Vitae** *n.* (Latin, 'Water of Life') The generic origin of distilled spirits. The most ancient written records show spirits had been distilled in simple alembic stills in pre-Medieval times, even in the regions of the world where no grapes were grown. One of the most colourful early references to the habitual use of spirits in the British Isles is that of Richard Stanyhurst who, in describing the nature of life on the 'island of Ireland' in 1577, quotes an ancient treatise by one Theoricus describing the qualities of the aqua vitae thus: '...it killeth the Flesh Worms...keeps the Hed from Whirlyng, the Tongue from Lispyng, the Mouth from Mafflyng, the teeth from Chattering, the Stomach from Wambling, the Guts from Rumbling, the Veynes from Crumpling and the Bones from Akyng'.

In Medieval Scotland, aqua vitae came to be regarded as a medical tonic, with its production and distribution coming under the control and strict licence of the Crown. It first official recorded reference comes in 1505 when Edinburgh's *Guild of Surgeon Barbers* was given a monopoly of the manufacture of Aqua Vitae purely for its medicinal purpose. However, by 1555 its popularity across Scotland for non-medicinal consumption was apparent from the number of breaches of the restrictions licence. Then, in anticipation of a bad harvest, a law was introduced restricting the use of grain and malt for making aqua vitae other than for the personal use of 'Earls, Lords, Barons and Gentlemen'.

**Arabia** *n.* In the annals of **alchemy** and distillation the Arabian origins of whisky must be recognised together with the those of ancient

Egypt, India and China. As civilisations merged on the European continent so the trade in herbs, spices, lotions and potions spread, taking with it the science of **alembic** distillation. In Arab culture the craft of alembic distillation of herbaceous liquors for perfumes and medicines was practised far and wide. Indeed we owe the existence of the word '**alcohol**' to its Arabic progenitor 'Al-kuhl'. The quest to perfect the crafts of **apothecary** and alchemy transferred across to Europe and was pursued across many cultures and communities in Medieval Europe. At the forefront were the monks and their religious orders who spread their influence by medicine and teaching and brought their apothecary skills into Ireland and Scotland.

**Arabinoxylan** *n.* Arabinoxylans are compounds found in the husks of grains believed to provide health benefits in bolstering the immune function and reducing cholesterol. Given the concentration of this matter in the **draff** residues of the mashing there is understandable value in collecting and recycling this draff as nutritious feedstuffs.

**Ardnamurchan** *n.* (Scots Gaelic, **Àird nam Murchan**) High ground of the seas. One of the new wave of small rural Highland distilleries. Founded in 2012 by specialist bottlers Adelphi, Ardnamurchan is the most western distillery on the British mainland with an annual production capacity of between 100,000-450,000 litres. Unusually, it released its first bottling as one year old new-make spirit before it had matured the required three years to become Scotch whisky.

**Arginine** *n.* An important amino acid present in the wort, rapidly absorbed from the very start of the fermentation. Some people suffer from a deficiency of arginine and may require to take it as a supplement. Arginine is naturally synthesised in the body and plays a key role in cell division, wound healing, removal of ammonia, immune defence functions and hormone production.

**Aroma** *n*. Our first sensory encounter with a whisky when it leaves the bottle and is poured into the glass. Swilling the spirit around the glass encourages the aroma to rise from the whisky and meet the nasal olfactory cells. A more detailed examination of the aroma can be undertaken by placing the nose over, and slightly into, the glass. First detectable observations should be the presence, or lack, of peat and smoke then depth and richness of the influence of the nature of the cask wood e.g. a former sherry or port cask, etc. A tip. Although it can attract a few odd looks, aroma is best assessed firstly with the eyes closed.

**Arran** *n*. Established in 1995, Arran Distillery was the first modern distillery to add to the long-established category of **Island** malt distilleries. For many years, this category was limited to Islay, Jura, Mull, Orkney and Skye. It now includes Arran, Harris, Lewis, Raasay and Shetland.

**Ash values** *n*. A measure of the presence of ash in the finished whisky derived from the charred wood membrane. This is measured to assess its possible influence as a flavour congener of any given sampling.

**Aspartic acid** *n*. A non-essential amino acid present in the wort. First identified in 1827, aspartic acid is an extract of asparagus juice and is one of the first group of amino acids to be readily absorbed at the beginning of the fermentation process.

**Assize** *n*. (Scots) Dating back to the 12$^{th}$ century, the assizes are the royally determined taxes and allowances placed on measurements of any produce applied to individuals and parishes. Also an old Scots measure of fourteen gallons.

**Atholl Brose** *n*. A traditional sweet Scots liqueur, made by mixing whisky, cream, honey, eggs and oatmeal. So legendary are its delicious and irresistible qualities that, in 1475, it was used as a lure to capture the rebel Iain MacDonald, Lord of the Isles. On discovering that the fugitive MacDonald supped nightly at a particular well, his pursuer, the 1st Earl of Atholl ordered the well to be filled with whisky, oatmeal and honey. Tasting this alcoholic ambrosia for the first time, Macdonald became intoxicated as expected. He lingered too long at the well and the tipsy but happy Lord of the Isles was easily accosted and captured by the waiting Atholl's men. Today Atholl Brose is a Hogmanay speciality, either as a welcome drink or a dram to see in the New Year. It is also a restaurant speciality served on its own or with mixers and cream topping.

**Attenuation charge** *n.* A government tax reckoned by **HMRC** against the quantity of alcoholic spirit capable of being produced from each tonne of malted barley in any distillery. The attenuation charge is calculated based on the proposition that one litre of alcohol is derived from every hectolitre of wort or wash. This reflects the efficiency of the yeast in consuming the sugars in the fermenting wort or wash and production of the by-products ethanol and $CO_2$.

**Auchlet** *n.* (Scots) An old Scots measure of dry barley or meal amounting to one eighth of a boll. In today's currency, this would equate to around 26.4 litres. The 'Aucht' element of the word, pronounced *Och-t,* is old Scots for eight.

**Auchtiken** (also **Auchtigen**) *n.* (Scots) An old Scots liquid measure. Defines one eighth of a barrel and one half of a firkin. In today's currency, an auchtiken amounts to around 25 litres of liquor.

**Auld Lang Syne** *n.* (Scots) Perhaps the most famous and universal of toasts voiced across the world and especially meaningful when raising a glass of whisky, meaning *the old days and old friends.* The poignancy of the toast to *Auld Lang Syne* is particularly apposite at the dawn of each New Year. Its humble celebration of folk and friendships past, as well as those here today, is recognised and shared across the world. Its sentiments were captured and immortalised in 1788 when Scotland's bard **Robert Burns** laid down this first verse and chorus from the famous song:

> Should auld acquaintance be forgot,
> And never brought to mind?
> Should auld acquaintance be forgot,
> And auld lang syne!
>
> *Chorus*
> For auld lang syne, my dear,
> For auld lang syne.
> We'll tak a cup o' kindness yet,
> For auld lang syne.

**Authenticity** *n*. Nowadays the true provenance and identity of any whisky is as important as the spirit itself. This is reflected in the prices collectors are willing to pay in today's worldwide premium whisky auctions and markets. As a result, forensic examination of whisky samples has become a much in demand specialist service, to identify and guarantee whisky authenticity and detect fraud. These examinations test for clear indicators that may disqualify the product as Scotch whisky. Forensic examinations concentrate on identifying any components that should be present in a particular brand and those components that should not be present. These include lack of maturation congeners or any traces in the whisky showing an age inconsistent with the stated age of the whisky. As an example, the presence of the flavour congener **vanillin** without its naturally occurring attendant maturation congeners would raise suspicion of a whisky's authenticity and origin.

**Azeotropic** *adj.* The process by which a complex liquid is separated into its pure components. In whisky distillation this occurs when **ethanol** and water become completely separated in the still as temperature causes evaporation of the ethanol. This is also known as dehydration of the ethanol.

Ben Averis
2017

# B

**Barley** 1: *n.* As the grape is to wine so the barley grain, or barley-corn, is to whisky. The four-rowed barley grain is the fundamental ingredient and source for brewing and distilling Scotch whisky. Through the centuries, barley varieties have been selected and refined to increase alcohol yield. Today the two-row barley variety with its higher sugar content is preferred with the alternative, traditional, six-row **bere** grain widely grown for food produc-tion. In agriculture, records from five centuries ago describe the harvesting, stoking and storing of barley grains across Scotland. The distilling process accesses the grain and its alcohol-producing sugars in the four stages of germination, fermentation, distillation and maturation. Barley is *malted* for whisky production. Over the centuries this process has evolved from small local malting barns and manual labour to large automated industrial malting plants. Nowadays most whisky produced in Scotland uses malted barley produced in these highly efficient bulk plants in vast Germination and Kilning Vessels (**GKVs**). This enables distilleries to plan their production around a constant and consistent supply of high yielding, quality malted barley. However, this large-scale production has also removed the 'terroir' bond between local distilleries and local barley producers in all but a few surviving malt brands.

2: *n.* (Scots) Any hand crafted alcoholic liquor made from malted barley. Also **Barley-bree, -brie, -broo**

**Barley-fetterer** *n.* (Scots) An old hand-held farming implement for stripping away the stiff bristles growing from the 'ear' of the barley flower.

**Barley-fever** *n*. (Scots) Euphemistic name for any illness or the display of odd behaviour brought on by sustained hard drinking.

**Barley-joke** *n*. (Scots) Distilled malt liquor, whisky.

**Barley-pickle** *n*. (Scots) The highest or topmost grain found on any ear of barley.

**Barley-sick** *adj*. (Scots) Any sickness or change in behaviour obviously attributable to overmuch drinking of whisky.

**Barley-unction** (also **Barley-auction**) *n*. (Scots) Any distilled malt liquor. Whisky.

**Barlic** (also **Barlic-hood, Barleyhood**) *n*. (Scots) A sudden fit of drunken, angry passion or aggression that is obviously fuelled by over-indulgence in whisky.

**Barm** *n*. The yeasty, scummy foam that builds up on top of the fermenting wash liquor in the washback. A by-product of the process of yeast converting the wort sugars into alcohol. Usually redundant waste in distilling, in brewing it can be used for kicking off the next fermentation of the new batch of liquor. Barm does have other uses, such as leavening bread in baking.

**Barrel** *n*. Crafted using either European or American white oak wood, the standard 195-litre oak barrel is the most commonly used vessel for maturation in Scotch whisky production. By a happy coincidence, the U.S. Bourbon Whisky Federal Standards of Identity regulations specify the 'single use' of new, charred 'American Oak' barrels by the American rye or corn whisky industry. These Bourbon regulations directly benefit the Scotch whisky industry in that they ensure a continuous supply of quality, charred barrels ready for filling with new-make spirit for maturation for three years and a day to become Scotch whisky. We also have to thank the Gauls of Northern Europe for inventing the oak barrel as a robust and dependable solution for storing, transporting and trading liquors and other general foodstuffs. As the Roman empire with its civilising traits moved north and west they faced key supply problems in supporting their legions with victuals. One challenge was the safe transportation of their brittle and fragile clay amphorae vessels containing wine in large quantities into landscapes with cooler, wetter climates. When they came upon the Gauls, in modern day northern France, they found people who had developed their own practical means of liquor transport by using wood bound together with metal hoops rather than clay. As ever the Romans tested this solution against their own and immediately found the benefit in adopting the wooden barrel for their precious cargo. Thus, the oak wood barrel became the European transport and storage vessel of choice for alcoholic liquor. It is a testimony to the early coopers of Gaul that little has changed in the design and manufacture of oak wood casks as its use spread across all continents of the world.

**Barrel-fevers** *n.* (Scots) Disorders and tremors of the body caused by excessive and extensive drinking of spirits. In modern parlance known as 'the shakes'.

**Barrique** *n.* (French) The most common style of wine barrel or cask, with a capacity of 225 litres. The Barrique is the default French cask size for maturing wine, also known as the Bordeaux barrel as the barrel was first designed and produced there. The Barrique's big cousin is the very slightly larger Burgundian **Piece**, which is more rounded and belly shaped.

**Batch** *n.* The traditional pot still method of whisky production in a distillery is also known as the batch process. Each spirit run produces a singular essence which is a unique combination of all the environmental variables and flavour influencers in that place, at that time within the framework of the distillery's style. These factors include temperature, the amount of interaction between vapour and the copper surfaces, intensity of reflux reactions and duration of each stage. It is also influenced by the source of the water, the productive qualities of the malted barley and the strain of yeast being used. All combine to produce a batch of spirit with its own distinct characteristics. This new-make spirit is now ready for the distillery's signature finishing and at least three years in the distiller's choice of oak cask.

**Bazil** *n.* (Scots) A habitual drunkard, a drouth, a sot.

**Bear** (also **Bere, Begg**) *n.* (Scots) The variety of four-rowed barley grain favoured for brewing and distilling.

**Bear-barrel** *n.* (Scots) The name of a traditional rural Scottish festival celebrating the successful completion of the barley harvest and the stooking of the cut barley in the fields for drying.

**Bear-curn** *n.* (Scots) A stone hand-mill or quern for grinding and manually de-husking batches of barley.

**Bear-land** *n.* (Scots) Any agricultural land specially set aside for the cultivation and cropping of barley. Also **Bear-feys**

**Bear-lave** *n.* (Scots) A traditional agricultural term for the condition of land in the first year after a crop of barley.

**Bear-mell** *n.* (Scots) A hammer-like implement with a wooden shaft topped with a rounded head of dense oak wood or stone. This hand-yielded tool was used to pound the barley grains held in the bear-stane. This bowl-shaped knocking stone held the grains for pounding to remove the husks and open the grain for accessing the meal or flour.

**Bear pundlar** (also **Bere-pundlar**) *n.* (Scots) The Orcadian name for the steelyard balance device used for weighing out quantities of barley.

**Bear-reet** *n.* (Scots) Agricultural land that was cropped for barley the year before.

**Bear-seed** *n.* (Scots) Barley grains at the time of sowing.

**Bear-stane** *n.* (Scots) The traditional hollowed, bowl-shaped stone used for manual grinding and de-husking of barley grains or bear by pummelling using the bear-mell.

**Beb** (also **Bebble, Bib**) *v.* (Scots) To drink liquor immoderately or carelessly. To swill, sip, tipple, brim over.

**Beir-corn** *n.* (Scots) A single grain of barley.

**Belly** *v.* (Scots) To drink deep and voraciously. To fill the belly.

**Bend** *n.* (Scots) A draught of liquor.
   *v.* To drink long and hard or greedily.

**Bender** *n.* (Scots) A solo, extended drinking session. Also someone who is a hard drinker. Someone who has become silly or buffoonish with drink.

**Benriach** *n.* From the Scots Gaelic **Beinn Riabhach**, the brown dappled Ben. This classic Strathspey distillery was built in 1898 by

John Duff during the railway boom period in the Highlands which saw 21 distilleries built along the Strath. Unfortunately, a bust period was close behind and soon rattling down the tracks. The distillery closed after just two years. Reborn in 1965, it has had a successful period as a creative, independent distiller bottling a wide range of peated and unpeated cask expressions.

**Bere** *n.* (Scots) The traditional Scots name for six-row barley grain variety. The earliest reference to bere cultivation dates back to the 8th century. Bere was chosen for its higher protein/nitrogen content compared to the two-row barley variety as it produces less fermentable sugar and is preferred for food production. In Scotland's Northern and Western Isles and on mainland Caithness bere is still cultivated as a food crop. This harvested crop goes for milling into *beremeal* for the production of traditional biscuits, bannocks and '*Aran-eòrna*', the Scots Gaelic name for barley bread. Two-row barley is believed to have been introduced to the British Isles by the Normans who valued its suitability for distilling and producing bread, beer, ale and whisky. In recent years, an Orkney brewery has used traditional six-row bere to create an ale, in Shetland a brewery has produced a beer and on Islay one distillery has created a bere malt whisky.

**Bitch-fu** (also **Bitch-fou**) *adj. and n.* (Scots) Aggressively, nastily drunk. Someone who becomes aggressive, difficult and objectionable when drunk. A beastly drunk.

**Blab** (also **Bleb**) *n. and v.* (Scots) A drop of liquor. To tipple. To slobber in drinking. making a gurgling noise when drinking.

**Blabber, Blebber** *n. and v.* (Scots) A tippler. To drink hard and often; *He's a right blabber him, he's aye blebbin and bitch-fou*

**Blabberin** (also **Blebberin**) *adj.* (Scots) Someone who is drunker than the rest of the company and at the extreme end of intoxication.

**Blash** *n.* (Scots) A large splash or a dash of liquid.
    *v.* To add too much water to whisky for the purpose of diluting. To drink or spill noisily and messily.

**Blawn-drink** *n.* (Scots) *Blown drink.* Liquor that is left over in a drinking glass or vessel filled and shared so that many have partaken and slurped thereof.

**Blaw-on** *n.* (Scots) A group participating in an unplanned but enthusiastic drinking bout. An impromptu drinking session.

**Blazin-fou** *adj.* (Scots) To be uproariously or mindlessly drunk.

**Bleed-raing** *n.* (Scots) An inflamed vein in the eye. *v.* To cause the eyes to become bloodshot.

**Blend** *n.* A blended whisky. Today a blend is defined in the Scotch Whisky Regulations as *a combination of one or more Single Malt Scotch Whiskies with one or more Single Grain Scotch Whiskies.* Blends are created using a carefully chosen core recipe combining between fifteen and forty distinctive single malts. These are added to the medium of usually two or three single grains to create a uniquely flavoured whisky which is given a colourful, non-distillery specific name. Blended whisky accounts for 90% of all the Scotch whisky shipped across the world. Today most of the world's best known blends are produced to the company's securely held original 'recipe' passed down through the years. Commercial blending of different whiskies to create a unique branded blend took off in the 1850s. The world's first marketed blend was *Usher's Old Vatted Glenlivet* launched in 1853. The larger distillers were producing high volume, cheap grain whisky using the Coffey/Patent process and realised the quality of their product and its price could be significantly enhanced by blending with the finer qualities of batched pot still malts. A good blend of between 15-40 different whiskies was found to produce a superior quality liquor to most single grain whiskies and blends became popular commercially.

*v.* To create a recipe which brings whiskies together and create a unique whisky taste and identity.

**Blended Grain** *n.* Whisky that is blended from two or more single grain whiskies from different distilleries. The Scotch Whisky Regulations require blended grain to be made only from Scotch whisky produced to the requirements of the regulations.

**Blended Malt** *n.* Defined in the Scotch Whisky Regulations as a blend of two or more single malt whiskies from different distilleries. This is also known as a vatted malt.

**Blender** *n.* A blender, or master blender, is a special person in a distillery whose skill, knowledge and sensitivity to whisky flavour and aroma has evolved and built up over many years. He or she possesses an intelligent nose and exhaustive knowledge of the aroma and flavour subtleties of hundreds of single malt and grain whiskies. Most blends combine anything from fifteen to forty single malts with two or three single grains in a malt to grain ratio generally between 20% and 40% of the finished batch. As with a master chef or orchestral conductor, the blender will be confident and creative in the selection of individual qualities and their special traits to interact and harmonise with each other. The blender will choose single malt and grain whiskies whose characteristics will come together to create a blend that is smoother, subtler and more complex than its individual elements. However, the blender cannot simply follow a recipe. The blend is an active process and small adjustments must be made during the vatting process.

**Blending Hall** *n.* A purpose-built area in a distillery where all the elements of the blending process are carried out. Under the direction of the master blender, selected casks are chosen for the blend and brought to the blending hall. These casks are individually sampled and 'nosed' to ensure they are of the required quality. If they meet the standard the casks are positioned over steel collection troughs, the bung removed and their contents emptied into the trough for filling into the blending vats. The whiskies are allowed a suitable period in the blending vat for settling. The master blender will occasionally draw out a sample to check for consistency. The Scotch Whisky Regulations specify that blending should take place using only whiskies which have been matured in oak casks for a minimum of three years and are legally defined as Scotch whisky.

**Blood Tub** *n.* Gloriously gory name for the smallest viable oak cask. With a capacity of just 50 litres, its small size harks back to more utilitarian times. Then transport of liquor across the Highlands was along horse and pony trails. Blood tubs are now seldom seen or used in general production.

**Blue** *n.* (Scots) Traditional colloquial name in north-east Scotland for peaty highland whisky.

**Blybe** *n.* (Scots) Any large quantity of strong spirits and particularly whisky.
   *v.* To take strong drink much and often.

**Boak** (also **Bouk, Bowk**) *n.* (Scots). A retch, vomit or involuntary belch. Used mostly when caused by over-indulgence in strong drink. The *Dry-boak* is a convulsive retch when there is no content in the gut to be vomited.
   *v.* To retch, vomit or belch.

**Body** *n.* The visible weight and liquid viscosity of a whisky once poured into the glass. Body can be assessed by firstly observing the movement and adhesion of the whisky as it is rocked and swilled around the bowl of the glass. The body of a whisky can be sensed more immediately and intimately as it is passed around the tongue and the mouth. One of the signature characteristics in assessing and tasting any whisky, body is generally classified in terms ranging from light and airy to dense and heavy.

**Boil Ball** *n.* The bulbous ball on the head of pot stills that causes intense interactions between the hot rising vapours and the copper surface. Also known as the **reflux**. As the liquor is heated to boiling point in the body of the still, the rising flow of hot vapours enters the boil ball of the reflux chamber. Here the vapour flow becomes disrupted and is recycled against the copper surface so that it cools, condenses and falls back down to be redistilled and vapourised again. This reaction within the still plays an important role in influencing the flavour of the whisky. The more intense the reflux chamber's interaction with the vapour, the lighter the taste notes to the spirit.

**Boinne** *n.* (Scots Gaelic, pron: *Bon-yeh*). A drop or droplet. A unit measure of liquid. Historically it is recorded that 60 *Boinnean* or droplets amounted to a **dram**. Nowadays a dram isn't measured in droplets but as a freestyle measure of poured whisky. The size of a dram varies depending on the generosity of the pourer. Its measurement in terms of size, quantity and value is a subjective matter of the recipient's opinion. Measurements can range from *measly* and *wee* to the less common, but more popular, *generous* and *bumper*.

**Boll** (Also **Bow**) *n.* (Scots) A unit of bulk measurement to quantify large consignments of dry flour or grain. Commonly used in Scotland until the 19ᵗʰ century. One boll was equivalent to around 211 litres or 64 pecks and not exceeding six bushels. In the late 1800s it was recorded in Edinburgh that a boll of potatoes was five hundredweights or 560 pounds. Scotland's Assize of 1618 created two distinct bolls. One measure was for wheat, pease, beans, rye and white salt, and a larger one for barley, oats and malt.

**Booze** (also **Bouse**) *n.* (Scots) Any alcoholic liquor or intoxicating drink.

**Boozy, bousy** (Scots) *adj.* Tipsy, fond of drink.

**Bordeaux Transport** *n.* A sturdy type of French or American oak wine cask of 300 litres capacity. Designed for bulk trading and shipping.

**Bottle** *n.* Standardised today as the 75 centilitre (75cl) capacity, clear glass model, the whisky bottle has evolved considerably from earlier vessels and containers. In the 17th and 18th centuries, recycling of glass bottles was a necessity in days when whisky was sold directly. Customers would turn up at their nearest hostelry/ dispenser/smuggler/merchant, often with a ceramic liquor jug, brown cow clay vessel or green glass medicinal bottle, looking for a refill of raw new-make spirit. Today's standard 75cl bottle size was established under EU regulation in 1993. This sought to bring order to the unregulated multiplicity of bottle sizing that existed across the continent in all the spirit, wine and liquor sectors and markets. These regulations also established other standard sizes of 1 litre (1L) and the miniature 5cl size.

**Bottling** *v. and n.* The filling and sealing of the finished whisky into a bottle and giving it a final labelled identity. In modern times this has become the defining moment when a whisky's long journey through the process of production and maturation stops. The largest Scotch Whisky bottling plant in the world is the Diageo plant at Shieldhall near Glasgow which ships over 26 million cases of whisky a year to 180 markets worldwide, amounting to around 25% of the total Scotch whisky exported annually. Once a batch of spirit has been

## Bourbon

matured and finished for the desired number of years the contents of the casks are sampled by the distillery manager, or malt master, to determine whether it is ready for bottling. Before bottling, cask strength whisky has its ABV brought down to an average 40%-45% by adding water. It may also then be then chill-filtered to extract the heavier oils and estery flavours which 'gauze' or cloud the whisky on pouring.

Increasingly with single malts the demand is for non-chill-filtered whisky. This preserves all the flavour elements, while some bottlings are also left at natural or cask strength. Very few distilleries bottle their whisky on site nowadays. Most send their finished whisky by road to be bottled at one the many specialist bottling plants in central Scotland.

**Bourbon** *n*. The classic American 'whiskey' named after Bourbon County, Kentucky where it was first produced. Just as a Scotch whisky has strict defining laws as to where and how it must be produced so rules also apply to American Bourbon whiskey. U.S. laws carefully define what can be called *Bourbon*. Currently there are ten distilleries in operation in the state of Kentucky; however, there is no legal requirement that Bourbon whiskey must be produced in the state. The law states that bourbon whiskey for US consumption must be: produced in the United States; distilled from a grain mixture that is at least 51% corn; distilled to no more than 80% ABV; aged in new, charred oak barrels; filled into the barrel for ageing at no more than 62.5% ABV; only water and no artificial colouring or flavouring can be added; and finally it must be bottled at minimum 40% ABV. Each bottle label must carry an age statement if bottled at less than four years old.

**Bourbon Barrel** *n*. Part of the legal definition for bourbon states it must be matured in new, charred oak barrels for a minimum of two years. This enables it to be called *straight bourbon*. But it may simply be called *bourbon* after maturing for just three months. Most bourbon brands however are bottled when the spirit has lain in the cask for between four and eight years. Scotch whisky has no such defined limit over the maximum age for maturation or number of times a cask can be used. Indeed, in Scotch whisky terms these casks are mere striplings and the intense flavour influences of the oak wood have only been lightly tapped at the surface membrane. So it is that a mutually beneficial market has grown between the two industries, whereby used bourbon casks find a ready value and price across the Atlantic. The majority of used American bourbon barrels are deconstructed for flat-packing and shipping across to Scotland where they are recoopered and filled with new-make Scotch whisky.

**Bran** *n.* When malted barley grains are ground into grist in the malt mill they separate into two elements. Bran comprises the fibrous husk material of the exterior and the flour which is resistant to breaking down in the mashing or cooking process. In the mashing the bran forms the major part of the porridgey draff residue left once the sugar rich wort liquid is drawn off. At the end of the mashing stage this is collected and dried for use as cattle feed.

**Brandy** (also **Brandy-wine**) *n.* The oak-aged distilled spirit derived from the Dutch *Brandewinj* or *gebrande wijn,* 'burnt wine'. The name reflects the test of the spirit readiness by setting a flame to it. This 'burning' of the finished spirit was to establish its quality at the end of its pot still distillation. Since grape is the basic ingredient it is natural that most brandy production areas in the world mirror the wine producing regions. In Europe only grape-derived spirit, matured for a minimum of six months in oak casks, can be called *brandy*. Known as Cognac in its traditional eastern European producing regions such as Georgia, the spirit is produced, like whisky, in a pot still process.

In many ways whisky's global penetration was made possible and even triggered by brandy's growing popularity in society across

## Brandy cellar

Europe in the 17<sup>th</sup> and 18<sup>th</sup> centuries. By the early 19<sup>th</sup> century it was well established in Great Britain as the spirit of choice in the upper echelons of society. Then a tumultuous series of natural catastrophes cleared the way for the ever-opportunistic Scottish whisky distillers to usurp brandy's pre-eminent position. It is believed this came about through the actions of English botanists who collected and brought to Europe specimens of American vines infested with the **Phylloxera** aphid nymph. The alien invader escaped and thrived, feeding on the sap in the roots of the nascent English vineyards whilst also injecting a deadly venom that killed the vine. The English vineyards were first to be infested and destroyed and soon an epidemic spread across the channel to France where in 1863 it was first recorded in the Languedoc wine producing region. The European grape harvest was devastated by the alien invader and between two-thirds and nine-tenths of European vineyards were devastated.

As a result, the continental production of wine and brandy crashed. Since the Phylloxera mites had no interest in barley, whisky production across Scotland continued apace unaffected. As the Brandy drought hit Britain the immediate availability of quality whisky in this time of emergency ensured it quickly took brandy's place as the spirit of choice across society. The Scots distillers recognised this opportunity, pursued it enthusiastically and ensured they entrenched their gains globally to establish Scotch whisky as the world's premium spirit.

**Brandy cellar** (also **Brandy-hole**) *n.* Any cave or underground place used by smugglers for concealing smuggled brandy. Their existence is recorded in an 1898 Ayr publication 'In the Olden Times no 203' by K Hewat who writes: 'In the dunes . . . between the village and the sea there are many 'brandy-holes' – spaces as large as an ordinarily sized room – where casks and bales landed from the smuggling vessel . . . were safely deposited'. (Dictionary of the Scottish Language)

**Brandy-cleek** *n.* (Scots) A paralysis and involuntary tremors or palsy of the leg believed in the 19th century to be brought on by hard drinking.

**Bree** *n.* (Scots) Any brewed alcoholic liquor, whisky, ale, etc.
   *v.* To brew, to drain liquid from solids that have been boiled.

**Breelish** *n.* (Scots) Any whisky at the strong ale or wash stage of the distillation.

**Brewer** *n.* The title often given to the person in the whisky distillery in charge of the mashing and fermentation stages. The name is an accurate description in that wash, the finished product from the wash room, is a form of beer, usually between 7-11% ABV.

**Brewing** *n.* The stage of the production process where the liquefied sugars in the cooked, malted barley, now called wort, are converted into alcohol by fermentation. This occurs in the wash-back fermentation chambers where yeast is added to the wort liquor. The yeast feeds on the sugars in the wort, producing alcohol and $CO_2$ as by-products and transforming the wort into a simple beer of 7-11% ABV.

**Broll** *n.* (Scots) A drinking pot.

**Broo** *n.* (Scots) Any brewed liquor or juice.

**Broo o'maut** *n.* (Scots) Whisky made from malted barley.

**Brose** *n.* (Scots) From the Scots Gaelic *Brothas*. The simplest form of making a meal using oatmeal, boiled water, butter and salt. Often prepared at night for the next day by leaving to stand overnight to allow maximum saturation by the liquid ingredients. **Atholl Brose** is a traditional sweet liqueur combining whisky, cream, honey, eggs and oatmeal. Usually served up as a Hogmanay speciality, as a welcome drink or as a dram to see in the New Year.

**Brown** *n.* (Scots) Any brown ale or porter.

**Brown cow** *n.* (Scots) A clay liquor vessel or jar.

**Browst** *n.* (Scots) A brew. The liquor produced by a brewing.

**Bucket** *n.* (Scots) A sarcastic colloquialism for a glass of spirits. Conversely also used to describe any over-indulgent quantity of alcohol.

**Bummock** (also **Bummack**) *n.* (Scots) A brewing of a large quantity of malt in one batch to provide enough fresh liquor for consumption at a special bash or a dance. Records from 1801 refer to 'as much as two bolls perhaps, appropriated for the purpose of being drunk at once at a merry meeting'. Also used to describe an obsolete Orkney tradition of tenants putting on a Christmas entertainment event for their landlords.

**Bunahabhainn** *n.* (Scots Gaelic) *Bun na h-abhainn* meaning 'the source or mouth of the river'.
    Three Gaelic words which describe the location of the Islay distillery that have been conflated into the single-word name used for this peated malt.

**Bung-fou** (also **Bung-fu**) *adj.* (Scots) Very comprehensively drunk, quite completely intoxicated.

**Burn** *n.* (Scots Gaelic, *Bùrn*) Water. (Scots) A small trickling stream.

**Burns, Robert** *n.* The most famous Exciseman in history is also Scotland's beloved national poet. As well as being celebrated as

Scotland's famous romantic bard and *bon viveur*, Burns (1759-96) took on the role of the Excise Officer for Dumfries in September 1789. His energy and enthusiasm in the post were such that he was soon promoted to the Dumfries Port Division on the very comfortable salary, for the time, of £50. It is recorded that he played a key part in the seizure of the whisky smuggling ship *The Rosamond* in March 1792 as it ran aground. The ship's contents were subsequently auctioned and, much to his superiors' outrage, Burns bought its four carronades and sent them to France, to aid the French Revolution. There is also evidence that he was not wholly comfortable with a profession for which he expressed his ultimate scorn in his poem 'The Deil's Awa wi' th' Exciseman' (the Devil has Taken the Exciseman).

> We'll mak our maut, and we'll brew our drink,
> We'll laugh, sing, and rejoice, man,
> And mony braw thanks to the meikle black deil,
> That danc'd awa wi' th' Exciseman.
> Chorus-The deil's awa, the deil's awa,
> The deil's awa wi' the Exciseman,
> He's danc'd awa, he's danc'd awa,
> He's danc'd awa wi' the Exciseman.
> There's threesome reels, there's foursome reels,
> There's hornpipes and strathspeys, man,
> But the ae best dance ere came to the land
> Was-the deil's awa wi' the Exciseman.
> The deil's awa, &c.

**Burst** *n.* (Scots) The occasional outbreak of an unplanned and impromptu drinking session.

# Cask

# C

**Cameronbridge** – see **Grain distilleries**

**Campbeltown** *n.* The first written reference to Campbeltown whisky dates back to 1591 and today it is one of the five Scotch whisky geographic **protected regions**. The region of Campbeltown comprises the South Kintyre peninsula ward of the Argyll and Bute Council but in reality Campbeltown malt whiskies are made within the boundaries of the town of Campbeltown itself. Campbeltown whiskies are characterised by their depth of flavour conveying distinctive sea salt notes on the palate. Prior to the coming of the railway in the late 19th century, Campbeltown thrived largely due to its advantage as a bustling seaport. It became the centre of West Coast whisky production with up to thirty distilleries operating on the Kintyre peninsula. But the town lost that advantage with the coming of the railway to Scotland. Freight transport largely shifted from sea to rail and many distilleries closed in the face of increased competition from the new inland distilleries built along the railway lines. Today only Springbank, Glen Scotia, and Glengyle remain in production. Springbank, founded in 1828, was built on the site of Archibald Mitchell's original illicit still. It remains in his family's ownership and is Scotland's oldest independent distillery. Uniquely, it continues to maintain all the processes and stages of whisky production from malting to bottling and labelling on a single site.

**Cap** (also **Cappy**) *n.* (Scots) A drinking cup. Small as in night cap, or larger cappie for use in a communal sharing.

## Cap out

**Cap out** (also **Cappie out**) *v.* (Scots) The act of drinking to the bottom of a vessel.

**Cap-stride** *n.* To deliberately pause or delay the passing round of the filled cappie to the next receiver by initiating pointless wittering, or needless chatter.

    *v.* A deliberate hold-up in the passing of the cappie.

**Caramel** *n.* The only colouring additive permitted in the production of legally defined Scotch whisky. The Scotch Whisky Regulations introduced in 2009 permit the use of a type of plain caramel colouring, namely E150a, to adjust the colour of whisky at the bottling stage. Under the terms of the Scotch Whisky Act of 2009, which sets and maintains production standards, Scotch is a spirit *'to which no substance has been added except water; plain caramel colouring; or water and plain caramel colouring'*. Increasingly, especially in the single malt sector, the addition of caramel is perceived as an unnecessary cosmetic infringement of a whisky's authenticity.

**Cask** *n.* The universal filling, storing and transporting vessel for Scotch whisky and most other wines, liquors and spirits. Of ancient design, relatively unchanged over two millennia, consisting of curved wooden staves and straw gaskets bound together with metal hoops. Scotch whisky casks must be made of American or European oak. Filling capacity is limited to 700 litres or less in order to ensure a consistent quality and standard of interaction between the spirit and the wood. There is no limit on the number of times a cask may be used for maturing Scotch whisky. Most commonly used casks in Scotch whisky production are American bourbon barrels holding around 200 litres and hogsheads with a capacity of 250 litres. Sizes increase to the sherry butts or puncheons with a capacity of 500 litres. Second use casks impart distinctive qualities. Sherry casks give a sweet, fruity character and a rich amber colour; Port pipes add deeper, darker colour and rich sweetness; wine casks produce a blush and a fruity, spicy nose. Casks of all types can be used multiple times, but after three or four refills the wood loses its vitality, integrity and its maturation powers. The wood also becomes increasingly permeable and to liable to the evaporation of the **Angels' Share**.

**Cask Finish** *n*. The distinctive flavour, colour and aroma of a whisky derived from the interaction between the spirit and the oak wood of the cask. After it has matured in the cask for three years and a day the spirit achieves its official *Scotch whisky* designation. It is now newly born Scotch whisky and can freely be poured to be enjoyed as such. However, most distilleries treat this point in the process as almost a second beginning, with the newly matured whisky now ready to be cask finished. Most single malt whiskies will mature in the original virgin oak or charred bourbon cask for at least six years. However, at some stage the distiller might also decide to transfer it to another cask for **finishing**. The new whisky is filled into specially selected casks to achieve a finish with distinctive characteristics. In these casks, the whisky will take on the distillers' signature characteristics in the distinctive flavour, colour and aroma acquired from the selected cask. Distilleries acquire and maintain a stock of used cask types across a range of ages and former uses for the particular flavours they have stored in the wood. Most commonly these have been previously filled with wine, sherry, port, and even other spirits such as rum. For example, a sherry cask will imbue a sweet, fruity character and a rich amber colour to the whisky while red wine casks produce a spicy character and a rose blush colour. Judging the length of time for finishing is a key skill in the distiller's art, as the longer the whisky spends in the finishing cask the more it will absorb its flavour characteristics. The distiller decides the optimum time for the finishing in terms of weeks, months and even years by balancing the influence of the cask against the characteristics of the original whisky.

# Cauld straik

**Cauld straik** *n.* (Scots) A dram of raw, cask strength spirit.

**Caulker** (also **Cauker**) *n.* (Scots) A bumper dram. A very large measure of whisky.

**Caup** *n.* (Scots) A wooden drinking vessel.

**Cellulose** *n.* The robust polymer compound characteristically found in all green plants, leaves, wood and the bark of trees. Cellulose fibres play a key role in holding together the cell walls and they are omnipresent in the oak wood of the cask. However, despite its extensive interaction with the maturing spirit, over time cellulose contributes very little in terms of flavour. Its only observable influence comes due to the application of high temperature in the charring of the cask. This enables a level of interaction with some carbohydrates to contribute a light toasting note.

**Change** (also **Change house**) *n.* (Scots) A tavern. An ale house.

**Change-keeper** *n.* (Scots) A licensed tavern or change house owner.

**Char** *v.* To apply direct flame to the interior of a cask to create charcoal. This substance is the dark and seldom seen presence lurking within the cask. All new casks are fired on the inside to char the surface. This opens the oak wood membrane, enabling the spirit to penetrate and absorb the wood's flavour tones. The blackened charcoal particles inside the cask contribute to a smoother, less fiery finish. At time of emptying the cask all charred particles are filtered out but their influence lives on in the bottle and the glass.

**Charcoal** *n.* Oak wood plays a complex role in maturation both in its natural condition and in its burnt condition as charcoal. In maturing new-make spirit, charcoal acts as an excellent filter.

Its presence in layer form on the inside of the charred cask and in particle form floating in the spirit extracts tangy components from the whisky. The charcoal particles in suspension will continue to influence the flavour of the whisky throughout its maturation. Casks are made ready for filling by firstly being fired or *charred* inside by application of direct flame. This breaks open the cellulose membrane allowing flavour compounds in the wood to react with the spirit. Nowadays the depth of the charcoal layer is recognised as an important factor in flavour and finish and is graded 1-4 when casks are being selected. We have to thank our American whisky-making cousins for discovering and perfecting the magic properties of charcoal in distilling whisky. The firing of casks began in the late 17th century as a sterilising measure for emptied casks that had been transporting food and organic contents for months across trails and rivers. When these charred casks were filled with whisky they were found to produce a finer, more mellow flavour than casks which hadn't been fired.

**Chaser** *n.* The traditional pairing of whisky and an ale as a two-drink combination, for drinking one after the other in quick succession. There is no strict order and having a 'whisky chaser' can mean drinking from the glass of ale after the whisky or drinking a shot from the whisky after supping on the ale.

**Chill filter** *v.* To remove heavier oil compounds from matured whisky. Chill filtering is the process of reducing the temperature of the whisky before bottling. The filtering then removes the haze-forming elements visible in the spirit at low temperature which cause clouding in the glass when water or ice are added. Chill filtration is common across all whisky categories as many consumers prefer their whisky to be clear. However, increasingly, there is a move towards non-chill filtered whisky as enthusiasts seek out authentic, original cask expressions.

**Ciuttie**

**Ciuttie** *n*. (Scots) A bowl of liquor. A measure of spirit or beer.

**Claggie** (also **Glaggy**) *adj*. (Scots) Gloopy. Soft and sticky. Used to describe a mash gone to thick sugary state.

**Clearic** *n*. (Scots) The distiller's name for the clear, still-strength, new-make spirit produced at the end of the spirit run and sampled in house. Until recently it was common practice for workers to receive a ration of clearic twice each day, during either half of their shift. This practice of workplace dramming on the production floor has now ceased. Ironically usually pronounced as in the ecclesiastical spirit-minded *cleric*.

**Coble** *n*. A boat-shaped tub or chamber for steeping malting barley.
    *v*. To steep barley.

**Cock-a-hoop** *adj*. (Scots) Well intoxicated. Half seas over. This is an older colloquial meaning. Nowadays it usually means 'exultant'.

**Coffey still** *n*. Dating from the 1830s and named after its inventor, Irishman Aeneas Coffey. Ironically, prior to becoming a distiller, he had been Ireland's Inspector General of Excise. Coffey took the basic continuous still process developed by Scotsman Robert Stein in 1827 and turned it into a vertical column model. Also known as the Patent still, the design uses two vertical columns which create spirit in a continuous flowing process. Internally, perforated copper plates divide the columns horizontally into chambers. The Coffey process begins with dissolving the starch in the unmalted cereals (such as maize and wheat) by cooking in converters under steam pressure. This is mixed with a 10%-15% measure of malted barley When yeast is added, the sugars ferment to create an alcoholic liquor of around 8% ABV. This liquor is sent to the first column, the Analyser, to be converted to hot spirit vapour (HSV). The HSV is then sent to the second column, the Rectifier. Here the heavier feints fall to the bottom while the refined spirit condenses near the top against the cold wash pipes. Grain spirit distilled by this method is usually run off at around 94.0% ABV, and then diluted to its casking strength of 63.5% ABV before being filled into oak casks for its three year maturation. Today this continuous method of distilling produces Scotch whisky on an industrial scale in the seven huge grain distilleries located around Scotland.

**Cognac Transport** *n.* A robust standard cask with a capacity of 350 litres, crafted from Limousin or American oak.

**Cold Finger** *n.* A feature of pot stills. Usually the **Swan neck** at the top of the still has a cold finger through which cold water can be channelled. This allows the still operator to chill any hot foam that might rise up the neck and otherwise find its way out of the still and into spirit forming in the condenser.

**Condenser** *n.* The heated ethanol vapours from the pot spirit are routed out via the lye arm at the top of the still into the condenser chamber. Here the vapours are funnelled into copper tubes chilled by cold water. This rapidly cools the vapours and returns them to liquid form. Being copper the condenser vessel also interacts with the vapour, contributing to the complex chemical reactions within the still system and influencing the flavour of the finished product. Often located outside the still house, condensers come in two different forms known as *tubes* or *worms*. The worm condenser is a long coil of copper tubing immersed in a circular tank of water, raised above ground level. The vapours are funnelled into the worm at the top and run off as condensed liquid at the bottom. The more efficient tube condenser works like a reversal of the worm. Standing vertically, the circular condenser chamber has cold water pumped through it via a dense cluster of copper tubes. The ethanol vapours from the still are funnelled into the chamber at the top where they cool against the pipes and reform as a liquid to flow out at the bottom.

**Congener** *n.* Congeners are signature influencing chemicals such as acetone, acetaldehyde, esters, tannins, and aldehydes produced in the distillation process. These are regarded as the source of such key sensory elements as the taste and aroma of the distilled spirit and ultimately the matured whisky. The volatile reactions and interactions inside the copper still produce these flavouring compounds as well as the desired ethanol and fusel alcohols.

**Coop** *v.* (Scots) To work on a cask. To hoop. To bind with metal hoops. Barrel-makers are called *coopers*.

**Copita** *n.* A tulip shaped stem glass, generally favoured and used in the tasting rooms of distilleries. The copita is chosen as it has an ideal shape for nosing whisky, being broad in its lower section to expose the spirit to the air and release the aromas, then narrowing to the brim, concentrating the aromas as they rise to meet the nose.

**Copper** *n.* One of the legally required signature elements of Scotch whisky. Pot stills are manufactured from copper for good reasons. As a metal, it is an excellent heat conductor and, being relatively soft, can be easily moulded and beaten into each distillery's characteristic still shape. It is also a key flavour influencer on the spirit, contributing flavouring complexities through its interaction and dissolution with the hot liquor and ethanol vapour. Finally, it also helps filter out unwanted compounds by attaching them during the volatile interactions inside the still.

**Cor, Friar John** *n.* The earliest known written reference to a batch of Scotch whisky is recorded in the 1494-95 Exchequer rolls. Dated 1st June, 1494 it reads: 'To Brother John Cor, by order of the King, to make *aqua vitae* VIII bolls of malt'. Brother John

Cor was a Tironensian monk, and Bailie of Lindores Abbey in Fife. The Tironensians were skilled alchemists and apothecaries, and Lindores Abbey is the most important historic site of pilgrimage for Scotch whisky lovers. King James IV granted the abbey rights to make *aqua vitae* to supply his hunting lodge at nearby Falkland Palace. The King favoured John Cor, gifting him fourteen shillings on Christmas Day in 1488 and black cloth from Flanders at Christmas time in 1494.

**Corn whisky** or **whiskey** *n.* Corn whisky or corn liquor is made primarily in the United States from a mash consisting of a minimum 80% corn and is distilled to 80% ABV. Corn whisky does not require to be aged and is bottled straight after distillation. Sold in this clear spirit form has led to it being known as 'white whiskey' or its popular soubriquet *White Lightning*. If matured in casks it must be diluted to below 62.5% ABV. If put into charred oak casks to mature, it falls under U.S. laws governing the production of Bourbon whisky and must be labelled as such.

**Counting dram** *n.* (Scots) The traditional shared dram of spirits poured to mark the payment of a bill and a settling of accounts between parties.

**Covenanter** *n.* (Scots) A traditional bell shaped ceramic whisky jar.

**Cowan, Jessie 'Rita'** *n.* Daughter of a Kirkintilloch doctor who came to be known as *the Mother of Japanese Whisky*. In 1920 against family wishes Rita secretly married her Japanese sweetheart, **Masataka Taketsuru**, at a Glasgow Registry Office and the couple left Scotland to follow his dream of making 'real' whisky in Japan. Masataka was soon utilising the knowledge and experience he had gained at the University of Glasgow and in his Scottish distillery apprenticeship to get Japan's first whisky distillery, at Yamazaki, running. Meanwhile Rita taught English and piano, immersed herself in Japanese culture and took Japanese nationality. Masataka finally established his own distillery in Yoichi, on Hokkaido. He chose this site because of its similarities to Scotland's west coast landscape and weather, being bounded on three sides by mountains and on the fourth by the Sea of Japan. Rita died in 1961, but the important role she played by his side in the distillery, and in the community, is reflected in the name of the main street in Yoichi: *Rita Road*. Their love story inspired a long-running Japanese TV drama and as a result Kirkintilloch sees many Japanese whisky enthusiasts who visit Rita's hometown.

**Cratur** *n*. (Scots) Another of the many Scottish nicknames, pseudonyms or aliases for whisky, derived from the Scots Gaelic **Creutair** meaning a living being of indeterminate form and either very good or very bad in character. Commonplace in Gaelic-speaking areas when differentiating whisky from other spirits such as rum or brandy. *Are you for a wee drop of the cratur?* is a common colloquialism when offering a dram of whisky.

**Cuach** *n*. (Scots Gaelic) A shallow Scottish drinking bowl or goblet – see **Quaich**.

**Cuilms** *n*. Tiny slender roots and shoots produced from the barley grain as it begins to germinate. In malting barley, the maltsters examine samples of the barley grains at this shooting stage and pay close attention to the quality of the cuilms. The speed of growth and length of the cuilms are key indicators of the likely production quality of the barley and its potential yield.

**Cut** *n*. The heart of the spirit. *Making the cut* is deciding when the qualities of the running spirit are perfect for making whisky, and before it has lost those qualities. The spirit run is divided into three elements: the **head**, the **heart**, and the **tail**, the heart being the fraction selected as fine spirit for final finishing in the cask. So, deciding when to make the cut is the most important moment in the still operator's shift. The rate of spirit run will affect the character of a distillery's whisky. Running the still fast will give a heavier, oily and sharper character. Running it slower produces a lighter, less intense spirit flavour.

**Cutty sark** *n.* (Scots) Traditionally a short underblouse and part of a woman's underlinen. Famously referenced in Robert Burns' celebrated poem *Tam O' Shanter*. When Tam salutes the bonny young witch dancing in the old Kirk of Alloway he cries 'Weel done cutty sark!' For over ninety years Cutty Sark has also been one of the best known and best-selling blended whiskies in the world using the image of the renowned *Cutty Sark* sailing clipper on its famous yellow label.

**Cutty stoup** *n.* (Scots) A small drinking vessel. A quarter measure.

A wee Dram
Conferencecall.net
Solitaire
Videos@home.net
Ben Averis 2017

# D

**Daniel, Jack** *n.* Jasper Newton 'Jack' Daniel (1849-1911) was the founder of the world-famous distillery in 1866 at Lynchburg, Tennessee, although official records suggest that the real date of founding may be as late as 1875. His immigrant grandparents were Scots, Welsh and Scots-Irish. Now owned by the Brown-Forman Corporation, Jack Daniel's charcoal filtered Black Label No 7 brand is established as the world's best-selling American whiskey, shipping over eleven million cases per annum. Although it meets the strict specification for classification as a straight Bourbon whiskey, the company has preferred to hold to its Tennessee Whiskey identity.

**Deil's Cup** *n.* (Scots) The Devil's cup. A particularly strong alcoholic drink.

**Deluxe blend** *n.* Premium blended whisky is distinguished by its combination of a high proportion of selected, high quality, aged malts together with well-matured premium grain whiskies. Normally a blend may combine the flavours of between fifteen and forty different whiskies with the malt element usually 20% or below. However, in any deluxe whisky the proportion of aged single malt is characteristically high and, in some cases, reaches 40%.

**Demi-Muids** *n.* A large double-sized hogshead shape finishing cask of 500 litres capacity made from American or European oak.

**Deoch** *n.* (Scots Gaelic) Drink. Also adopted by English speakers across Scotland as the colloquial name for any alcoholic drink. Usage is especially popular in the Highlands and Gaelic-speaking communities. *On the deoch* is traditionally used as a euphemism for a sustained bout of drinking.

**Deoch an dorus** *n.* (Scots Gaelic) From the highland tradition of the *deoch aig an dorus*, literally the *drink at the door*. Also known as the parting glass, the leave-taking glass and the stirrup cup. The pouring of a last dram for visitors about to leave at the end of a house visit or ceilidh. The tradition was famously immortalised and taken round the world in Sir Harry Lauder's music hall song *Just a Wee Deoch-an-Doris* (sic). Written and composed in 1911 by Sir Harry, Whit Cunliffe and Gerald Grafton, the song explains the custom thus:

> There's a good old Scottish custom that has stood the test of time.
> It's a custom that's been carried out in ev'ry land and clime.
> Where brother Scots foregather
> It's aye the usual thing.
> For just before they say "Good Nicht," they fill their cups and sing
>
> *Chorus*:
> Just a wee deoch-an-doris,
> Just a wee yin, that's a'.
> Just a wee deoch-an-doris,
> Before we gang awa'.
> There's a wee wifie waitin',
> In a wee but-an-ben;
> If you can say, 'It's a braw bricht moonlicht nicht,'
> Then ye're a' richt, ye ken.

**Deoch-bhleith** *n.* (Scots Gaelic) Literally the grist dram. By custom the fourth dram taken in the highland tradition of *four drams of the* *morning* after waking and waiting on breakfast. Deoch-bhleith is the final dram before lunch.

**Deoch-eòlais** *n.* (Scots Gaelic) The first drink on first meeting a stranger. The getting-to-know dram.

**Deoch-lag** *n.* (Scots Gaelic) Weak drink. Any soft drink.

**Deoch–làidir** *n.* (Scots Gaelic) Strong drink. Alcohol. Spirit.

**Deoch slainte!** *n.* (Scots Gaelic) Commonly used traditional toast, celebrating and wishing good health.

**Devil's cut** *n.* The portion of spirit that soaks deep into the oak wood of the cask and stays in the cask when it is sent for emptying of its contents for bottling. The spirit penetrates deep into the oak wood in its original cask fill strength and is stored in a layer. The amount and depth of spirit trapped in the Devil's cut is influenced by average air temperature, humidity and quality of the wood. Although trapped, this rich flavour complexity is not lost forever if the cask is used again. New spirit filled into the cask will penetrate the Devil's cut layer and recover its potent flavour influences.

**Dist** (also **Sids**) *n.* (Scots) The husk of the barley grains separated from the floury starch in the milling.

**Distil** *v.* To create a liquor in a metal chamber by application of heat to cause purification and evaporation and applying cold to cause reformation as a liquid. The origins of distilling belong in the ancient crafts of alchemy and perfumery. In the 7th and 8th centuries, Arab and Chinese cultures would boil rose petals and pungent flowers in alembic chambers to capture and extract their aromas. These skills were much sought after and the products were valued commodities. The first recorded distillation of alcohol for drinking from wine is accorded to the *Aqua Vin'* produced by the Majorcan polymath Ramon Lull (1236-1315) and his teacher **Arnold de Villa Nova**. Lull demonstrated his passion and creativity by fermenting his wine for twenty days in horse dung before distilling the wash into a basic condenser. These pioneers recorded their exuberance at the heavenly qualities of the taste and aroma of the distilled wine they produced, describing its taste as 'elixir and a panacea that humanity had long been waiting for.'

With its vast, continuous supply of wine, France was a natural cradle for this developing craft and distilled wine in the form of French brandy became much sought across the continent. In the harder climes of northern Europe, the grape was much less productive. So it was that those with substantial grain harvests took to the making of spirit with some of their store. In the British Isles, the monastic spread of Christian scholastic science and knowledge brought the production of medicinal **aqua vitae**/water of life/ **uisge beatha** to Scotland and Ireland. It soon became widespread. In Scotland, the earliest written reference to a batch of Scotch whisky is found in the 1494-95 Exchequer rolls. Here it states that **Brother John Cor**, Tironensian monk of Lindores Abbey and a skilled alchemist and apothecary is granted rights to make aqua vitae to supply the king's hunting lodge at nearby Falkland Palace. Lindores Abbey is now a site of pilgrimage for Scotch whisky lovers.

**Dog** *n*. So named due to its attached *lead* and the fact that it is traditionally a distillery worker's constant companion. This test-tube shaped brass vessel is crafted to the exact measurements of a whisky cask bung hole, designed for dipping into the very same. Its weight ensures it sinks and fills with a good measure of whisky to be lifted for sampling. An essential tool for those concerned with the very important role of monitoring quality and taste during the maturation process. Handily, the slim nature of the dog's design enables it to be carried unseen in the fold of a jacket or well-tailored trouser leg. Significantly, it is also known as the **Thief**.

**Donald** *n.* (Scots) A Donald is a traditional Scots colloquialism for a pouring of an exceptionally generous draft of whisky. Truly. Exceptionally generous. So, so bigly, bigly generous…

**Draff** *n.* The thick sludgy residue of husks and solid matter left in the base of the mashtun after the mashing process. Draff has long been used as a nutritious sugary animal feed after being dried and bulked into a saleable form. Once the sugary wort is drawn off at the fermentation stage, the remaining porridgey mass is cleared away through drain holes by rotating the Lauter blades. The draff is then pumped at high pressure, either into a draff receiver chamber or a wagon waiting outside the mash room for transport to a processing plant.

**Draff-sack** *n.* (Scots) A sack or pock for holding, storing or transporting dried draff, the residue produced after the waste from the mashed malted barley has been dried and reduced to grains.

**Draffy** *adj.* (Scots) A liquor of inferior quality having been brewed from the leftover draff or residue of the mashing of the malted barley.

**Dram** *n.* (Scots Gaelic) A single poured measure of whisky. The origins of the dram and its evolution lie in the improvement of the quality and supply of distilled whisky in the late 18th century. This increasing availability of quality whisky in change houses in the rapidly growing cities of the era made it a popular addition to beer, wine and port. The pure malt spirit produced for sale had so improved that drinkers were now choosing to drink an unmixed or undiluted dram measure. This amounted to 1/3 of a pint of cask strength 60% ABV whisky. Another measure of the dram originates in a definition that records it as consisting of 60 boinnean or drops of the spirit. Nowadays the measure of a dram is no longer calibrated so exactly in droplets. Instead it is rather an expression of the generosity of the pourer. The judgement of the measurement is a matter of the recipient's opinion. Most commonly heard dram measurements are 'measly' and 'wee'. Less common but more popular dram measures are 'huge' and 'bumper'.

**Drambuie** *n*. From the Scots Gaelic *dram buidheach* 'the satisfying dram' or *dram buidhe* 'the yellow dram'. The famous whisky liqueur is reputedly made from the personal recipe of Prince Charles Edward Stuart or Bonnie Prince Charlie (1720-88), who is said to have passed the secret recipe to Skye man John Mackinnon in gratitude for Clan Mackinnon's protection following the catastrophic defeat at Culloden in 1746. The recipe was acquired by Broadford hotel owner John Ross, in 1873, who made batches for consumption by his hotel guests. Local enthusiasts gave it the Gaelic name which became shortened, when Anglicised, to Drambuie. The name was later registered by his son James Ross but it was another Skye man, Malcolm Mackinnon, who got permission from the Ross family to manufacture it commercially in Edinburgh in 1909. By 1914 he had acquired the trademark and rights from the family and formed the Drambuie Liqueur Company. Mixed with whisky, Drambuie is the key ingredient in the Rusty Nail cocktail.

**Dram-glass** (also **Copita**) *n*. (Scots) A fine, tulip shaped glass popularly used at whisky tastings for sampling newly poured whiskies. The wide base and tall, narrow neck of the glass channel the aromas to the nose and mouth.

**Dramming** *v*. (Scots) The communal or group sampling of specially chosen whiskies for the purpose of sharing tasting notes and opinions. Any informal gathering around a bottle of whisky where drams are dispensed to punctuate the sharing stories and enjoying the craic until the bottle is finished.

**Drap** (also **Drappie**) *n*. (Scots) A small shot, a one-off dram. Literally 'a drop'. Another colloquial euphemism for a measure of whisky.

Commonly said when wishing to disguise the pouring of a large or generous measure of whisky in the presence of disapproving non-whisky drinkers. The size of the pour can be further camouflaged by prefixing it with *Wee*, *Just a wee...* or *A toaty wee...*

**Drap o'dew** *n.* (Scots) Any small dram or small pouring of whisky.

**Dreeple** (also **Dripple**) *v.* (Scots) To trickle or dribble spirit down the outside of a vessel.

**Dreggle** *n.* (Scots) A small pouring. A drop of liquor.

**Dreggy** *adj.* (Scots) Murky, cloudy or opaque spirit, suggesting it has been poured last. Liquor from the bottom of the barrel.

**Dregs** *n.* The remains at the bottom of a bottle. On a larger scale, the residue left in the still. In grain distilleries using continuous patent still distillation this fine grain sediment left at the bottom of the analyser is flushed away to cool and settle in dregponds. The liquid eventually drains away and the remaining sediment is dried and transformed into animal feed.

**Drib** *n.* (Scots) A small spot or splash of liquor.

**Drift-line** *n.* (Scots) A concealed, submerged anchor line used along the seashore to attach to 'smuggled' kegs. Used during the times of the whisky wars in the 19th century, these filled kegs were hidden a few feet beneath the surface of the sea, beyond the tide line using weights. When the coast was deemed clear and free from the eyes of the Excise officers, the sunken casks would be retrieved and spirited away for delivery to expectant customers.

**Drin** (also **Drins**) *n.* (Scots) A drop or drops of water added to liquor.

**Drink-siller** *n*. (Scots) Drink money, a tip passed across the counter.

**Dripple** *v*. (Scots) To dribble or trickle. To drip a liquor.

**Drouk** *v*. (Scots) To soak or steep in water to trigger germination in grains.

**Drouth** *n*. (Scots) A compulsive drinker, a thirsty person, a tippler, a drunkard. An intense dryness of throat arising the morning after a bout of sustained drinking. A thirst that demands intense and immediate hydration relief through drinking copious amounts of water. A drought.

**Drouthelie** *adv*. (Scots) Thirstily, quenchingly.

**Drouthiesome** *adj*. (Scots) Given to drinking regularly and steadily.

**Drouthiesomeness** *n*. (Scots) An addiction to regular drinking.

**Drow** *n*. (Scots) A very small quantity of liquid, a drop.

**Drown** *v*. To commit the social gaff of publicly diluting a whisky beyond its identifiable taste. To add so much water that it masks a whisky's true character and spoils its whiskiness.

**Druck** (also **Drucken, Druckensome**) *adj* (Scots) Drunk, drunken.

**Drucken-bite** *n*. (Scots) Food served up in drinking premises of a kind likely to encourage patrons to stay on and consume more liquor e.g. dried seaweed, pickled eggs, pork scratchings.

**Drucken-groat** *n*. (Scots) Money paid by into the fund to buy the drink by those attending at a penny-wedding. A fine for drunkenness. The credit bill run up by regular customers with a drink seller.

**Drums** *n*. The use of rotating maltings drums, as opposed to fixed steeping vats or vessels, was developed as an efficient method of malting smaller batches of barley. The use of small drums particularly suited whisky smugglers, as they were transportable. This enabled the smugglers to produce malt anywhere they chose to set down rather than solely in fixed location steeping tanks.

**Drunken-fu** *adj*. (Scots) Full of drink, to the point of being well adrift from the level of sobriety of the rest of company. A person or persons clearly drunker than his/her/their companions.

**Dry-moud** *adj*. (Scots) Dry-mouthed. The non-partaking of available alcohol. Going without. The lot of the designated driver. Being completely sober while stuck in a company of enthusiastic, ribald and increasingly intoxicated friends out on the spree.

**Dunnage** *n*. The traditional warehousing method for stacking filled casks on top of each other during the spirit's maturation. The name reflects the loose wooden duns, or joists, which are placed manually between each layer of casks and piled to three layers high in the warehouse. Dunnage warehouses are built with thick stone walls and earthen floors which help maintain an even humidity. Although labour-intensive, the dunnage method of storage is retained as an important option for maturing in many distilleries. Most modern warehouses are built to much larger dimensions with stronger steel racking allowing many more layers for storage and larger capacity on palletised systems. These differ significantly from traditional cask storage by stacking casks on their end side by side on pallets.

# E

**Edradour** *n.* From the Scots Gaelic ***eadar dhà dhobhar*** meaning 'between two rivers'. Founded in Pitlochry in 1825, Edradour was generally recognised as the smallest traditional distillery in Scotland, until the arrival of small craft distilleries in the 21st century. Two distillery workers produce 18 casks each week amounting to a modest distillery output of 95,000 litres each year.

**Effluent** *n.* Not all co-products from the production process can be put to beneficial and commercial use. Draff cattle feed and fertiliser account for most of the material with commercial nutritional or organo-chemical value. However, a quantity of residues and effluents have no further value. Pot ales, spent lees, washing waters and syrups may be disposed of in a variety of ways depending on local circumstances. In coastal and island locations disposal to estuary and sea along a long outfall pipe is permitted with strict environmental monitoring. Inland, reed lagoons and dreg ponds can organically filter and dissipate effluent to the atmosphere and ground water. Another agricultural solution is tractor-tankering the diluted effluent to spray-irrigate over fields in surrounding areas.

**Enzyme** *n.* A protein occurring in living plant grains which, in certain pH, temperature and moisture conditions, will catalyse a key metabolic change. In distillation, this important metabolic change triggers the conversion of starch stored in the malted barley into sugars. The most important enzymes in the breakdown of the starch molecules for sugar conversion are the alpha-Amylase and beta-Amylase enzymes. These perform most efficiently in the mashing at a consistently maintained temperature of 64.5°C.

**Esters** *n*. Esters are a group of **flavour congeners** which contribute the lighter flavours of a whisky and are produced together with alcohols and acids within the yeast fermentation and on the copper surface of the still. Flavour congeners influence the taste of the whisky and, in the case of *estery* whiskies, the taste characteristics are often described as: fruit, wine, perfume, lemonade and pear drops.

**Ethanol** *n*. The official name and chemical definition of **alcohol** as agreed at the International Conference on Chemical Nomenclature in Geneva in 1892. Ethanol is first produced in the whisky-making process as a by-product of the fermentation of the sugar-rich wort in the wash-backs. As the yeast feeds and grows on the sugars it produces the desired soluble ethanol in the wort and vast quantities of $CO_2$ which must be vented from the chamber to the open air if it cannot be commercially collected. The yeast dies off once it has exhausted all the sugars in the wort. The transformed liquor **wash** is a simple, fresh citrus-flavoured beer with an alcohol by volume (ABV) content of 7-11%.

**Evaporation** *n*. All whisky makers feel a great sense of satisfaction as another oak barrel is filled with 200 litres of new-make spirit. As the bung is hammered in there is a warm glow that the wood and spirit will now begin their journey over the years to create a beautiful marriage and a unique tasting whisky. Unfortunately, the years also take their toll on the 200 litres. In the Scottish climate, it is estimated that 1% of the volume of spirit evaporates through the wooden cask each year to hang in the air of the bonded warehouse as the **Angel's Share**. The treasured 50 year old malt whisky is bottled from its cask with the sad knowledge that as much as 100 litres of this beautiful crafted and curated whisky has 'left the building' and simply evaporated. Even worse, down under, in the award winning whisky production regions of Tasmania the humidity and air temperature fluctuations mean that the Angel's Share can sometimes be as high as 7% per annum.

**Excise** *n.* In 1664, the Scottish government recognised that there was substantial income to be gathered from the legalisation of the widespread illicit production of *uisge beatha*. The Excise Act was introduced as the first of the many Acts of Parliament devised to extract crown revenue from the widespread production of the spirit across the land. This placed a new tax of two shillings and eight pence to be levied on every pint produced. The cost-effectiveness of this money-gathering scheme is reflected in the fact that a new crown enforcement service was created to ensure the government's coffers and interests were dutifully observed. Government officers were appointed and charged with chasing down illegal distilling and revenue collecting. The **Exciseman** was born! Out in the country a new era of smuggling dawned as this new bogey man began to stalk the hills and glens of Scotland. Further government control of production in distilleries saw the creation of the **spirit safe** in every distillery and its keys in the hands of the ever-present Excise Officer.

**Excise Officer** *n.* The role of the Excise Officer or Exciseman or (Scots) **Gauger** has been twofold down through the centuries. Their primary duty is to ensure all legal distillers account for the spirit they produce and pay the appropriate level of duty. Their secondary duty is to ensure that no illegal distilling or smuggling of whisky takes place anywhere in Scotland and, if it does, the perpetrators are brought to justice. This proved to be a challenging task, particularly in the 18th century when Excise officers acted almost as an independent paramilitary police force in rural areas of Scotland, where they were often reviled by the local community. Tacit support for the smugglers and illegal distillers went right to the topmost layer of society. The local landowners were often their most important clients and Excise officers might haul smugglers before a local Justice of the Peace for judgement - who happened to be one of the smugglers' prime customers!

By the 19th century, Excise Officers had an observation office in each distillery with keys to the spirit safe and were required to live in a house nearby. This didn't help with local popularity and they often made pragmatic allowances for obvious production discrepancies for the sake of a peaceful life. Scotland's most famous Exciseman was its beloved national bard, **Robert Burns**. Appointed as the Excise Officer for Dumfries in September 1789 he took up the role with energy and enthusiasm and was soon promoted to the Dumfries Port Division on the very comfortable salary, for the time, of £50. Whatever his enthusiasm for the role he expressed his ultimate disdain in the poem *The Deil's Awa wi' th' Exciseman* (the Devil has Taken the Exciseman).

# F

**Feints** *n.* The last portion of the spirit run in the final stage of the second distillation is too dilute and low in alcohol to be suitable for making whisky, lying in the range 30-35% ABV. The volume of liquor run off as feints amounts to about 40% of the original charge but contains heavier alcohols and residual oily components too pungent to be included in the batch. Feints aren't discarded but are drawn off through the blue pipe to be combined with the foreshots in the feints receiver for recycling. In the next charge of the still, this mixture plays an important role in starting the next batch while retaining and conveying signature flavour characteristics from the previous batch.

**Fermentation** *n.* The vigorous brewing stage which takes place in the washback vessels. The sugar-rich wort being is filled into the brewing vats at a temperature range between 19 and 22°C depending on seasonal average. Fermentation is then triggered by adding one kilo of moist yeast per 1000 litres of wort. Thus begins the volatile fermentation as the yeast converts the sugars into ethanol. Over the first 24 hours, this reaction produces $CO_2$ as a by-product and creates a rising temperature which cannot exceed 34°C as this will kill off the yeast. A normal fermentation cycle runs between 48 to 56 hours and stops naturally when all sugars are converted to ethanol and the yeast dies. Some distillers may leave it as long as 72 hours over a weekend. The fermented liquor in the washback, now a pale cloudy alcoholic beer of around

**Ferintosh**

7-11% ABV, is piped through to the still room to begin the first distillation.

**Ferintosh** *n.* (From the Scots Gaelic; ***Fearann Toisigheachd*** also ***Fearann Tòisiche***). *Lands of the founders, prince or thane.* Situated in the Highlands around the Cromarty Firth, Ferintosh is recognised by many as the site of the oldest legal distillery in Scotland. In 1689, the landowner of the lands of Ferintosh was Duncan Forbes of Culloden. By way of his political allegiance, Ferintosh was granted a unique status amongst Scotch whisky distillers as Scotland's first legal distillery. Forbes was granted a royal exemption, given in perpetuity to his family successors, from payment of any duty on the distillation of his *aqua vitae*. However, as a notable Highland Whig, Forbes had made himself unpopular with Jacobites through his support for William of Orange in the Glorious Revolution of 1688. The Roman Catholic King James II was ousted and in the aftermath the Jacobites rallied in support of the deposed king by sacking Forbes's Ferintosh estate and razing his brewery and distillery to the ground.

Forbes lodged a damage compensation claim with the Scottish Parliament for £54,000 and, in response, the parliament granted that he and his descendants be forever allowed to distil grain from his own lands, free from any duty in return for an annual payment of 400 merks Scots, roughly equivalent to £280 Scots. The offer was duly accepted and soon the quality of Ferintosh whisky distilled at Ryefield on Gallow's Hill above Dingwall became renowned across Scotland. By the 1770s Forbes's Ferintosh base had expanded to four more distilleries producing 90,000 gallons and profits of £18,000 annually. However, it all came crashing down in the late 18th century when the other entered or illegal distillers become so frustrated by Forbes's unfair advantage they successfully lobbied in 1784 to have the duty- free status of Ferintosh rescinded.

The additional financial burden was too much and the distillery closed within a year.

**Finish** *v.* To select and fill the final cask for the whisky's maturation. The defining maturation stage producing the final flavour and character of any whisky. Also, the lasting flavour or aftertaste in the mouth on drinking a whisky. After three years in the cask the spirit is legally whisky but its maturation journey is by no means over. Whisky takes between five and eight years to truly mature, so that all metallic taints are gone and the spirit enters its final flavour stage. Having reached its full maturity, the whisky takes on its distillery or '**terroir**' identity. The distiller now has options as to where to take this whisky by adding flavours, colour and aromas from selected oak casks. The choice of finishing cask is key in adding the distinctive taste and colour finish characteristics such as the rich and fruity European oak casks that previously held a range of wines, port and sherries. By keeping the spirit in these first fill casks for between twelve weeks and two years the base whisky is given the distinctive mark of the distiller that makes it stand out from the crowd.

*n.* The finish also describes the final taste, tones and flavours left on the palate after the whisky has been savoured and swallowed. A finish in any good whisky should be complex, changing and long lasting. It should inspire flowery descriptions such as: *a strong smoky finish, a light aromatic vanilla finish with almondy aftertaste, a bright finish of smoked salmon, strawberries and sodden leather boots*...and so on.

**Flavour** *n.* The final flavour of any whisky is a confection of many influences. It emerges in the cask following the germination, fermentation, distillation, and maturation processes. Starches, sugars and compounds interact with water, yeast and temperature, to enhance the primary flavouring influences created in the distillation: esters, aldehydes, oils, sulphides and woods. The new-make spirit has a schnapps type flavour which it loses as it matures in oak casks and, over time, takes on the characteristic flavours of the wood. It is generally agreed that as much as 70% of the whisky's final flavour is derived from the cask.

**Flavour Congeners** *n.* Chemical compounds arising in the most volatile interactions produced in the distillation reflux. These are reckoned to be responsible for most of the taste and aromas in a whisky. Boiling the wash in the pot still produces the ethanol and fusel alcohols which interact along with the other flavour congeners including acetone, acetaldehyde, esters, tannins, and aldehydes. These compounds are also believed to be the signature contributors to hangover symptoms and, more morbidly, are used by forensic toxicologists *post mortem* to determine what a person drank.

**Flavour threshold** *n.* The point during maturation at which any flavour is deemed to have contributed its maximum to the spirit. From the time of filling, the new-make spirit starts interacting with the wood. In doing so it gradually absorbs flavours and colour from the breakdown and synthesis of the wood sugar compounds. These new flavour elements, or congeners, permeate the spirit until they reach their *flavour threshold*. This happens at different times in the maturation process depending on their complexity. For example, the flavour congener **vanillin** in oak wood is reckoned to reach its maximum flavour threshold after just six months.

**Flavour Wheel** *n.* At first glance visually complex, the flavour wheel is an intuitive, easy to use, visual aid for whisky professionals and enthusiasts alike. Using overlaying segments and categories, it enables samplers to identify groups and origins of flavours and analyse the characteristics in a whisky. Ranging from small, simple and easy to carry around to poster-sized works of art, flavour wheels map the spectrum of taste and flavour attributed to specific components. These help tasters to understand

and analyse their own sensory reactions to nosing, tasting and aftertaste.

**Foreshots** *n*. The first fifteen to thirty minutes of a spirit run is too raw to be of potable quality. The volume of foreshots run off is around 5% of the low wines and feints charge. This head of spirit contains heavy oils and esters from the previous distillation detached from the copper surface of the still and condenser. Foreshots contain too high a proportion of volatile, flavour influencing compounds which show up as verdigris colouration as it runs through the spirit safe. The still operator diverts the foreshots through a blue pipe to the feints receiver for mixing at the end of the spirit run. He also determines when the cut point for the potable heart is reached by the **water test**. This involves mixing water with a sample of foreshots in the spirit safe. At first the mix appears milky and turbid. When it shows clear, the spirit is deemed potable. This is now the potable heart of the spirit and the still operator will divert the run for collection in the spirit receiver.

**Fou** (also **Fouish, Fu**) *adj*. (Scots) Filled to repletion. Intoxicated, drunk.

**Fraction** *n*. Though continuous, a spirit run is nominally broken into three distinct fractions. These are described as the foreshots (or head) the middle cut (or heart) and the feints (or tail).

  **Foreshots** comprise the first 5% of the run and are collected for around the first 20 minutes of the second distillation. Highly volatile compounds, they must be excluded from the final spirit. The **middle cut** is the best of the spirit and consists of around 15% of the clearest spirit run. The weak and tainted **feints** account for the next 40%. These are run off to be mixed with the earlier collected foreshots and used in the start of the next distillation. Finally, the last fraction is the **spent lees**, accounting for the last 40% of the spirit run. This is treated as a by-product, to be re-oxygenated in reed ponds or sprayed over agricultural fields. The stillman's most important and influential decision is when to make the cut. That is, to select the purest fraction of the spirit run as the middle cut, or heart. At this point, he splits the fractions by switching the pipe run. Selecting only the best of the spirit is key to determining the eventual quality of any distillery's whisky.

**Fraser Yew** *n.* The Fraser yew tree has a special place in the history of whisky and the Highlands. High on the steep south banks of Loch Ness, near Loch Knockie, lie the lands of the Loch Ness sept of the Fraser clan. When the Frasers arrived in the area around the 14th century they took to meeting beneath an ancient yew tree which at that time may already have been 1,000 years old. Over the centuries, the girth and spread of the tree had created a vast green dome of branches, encircling and enclosing a space within which up to 100 clansmen could gather unseen, and it became the natural gathering place for the Frasers of Stratherrick and Knockie.

It was also adopted as the clan's plant symbol so that, before a battle, they'd carry a sprig of yew in their bonnets to symbolise kinship and loyalty to each other. Another of the great traditions of meeting within the yew for these clan parliaments was the ritual sharing of whisky. Today the Fraser yew is more than thirty metres in diameter and still growing at an estimated 1,600 years old. While the original grandmother trunk is hollowed and moss-covered, its daughters, granddaughters and all its direct offshoots form a vibrant natural screen around it. A unique principle of Highland hospitality also lives on here in the Clan tradition of providing a warming dram to visitors beneath its branches. In this the Fraser yew is unique amongst trees, with its unbroken history of providing whisky to those who stop to contemplate the nature and history of this ancient living thing. Be they clan pilgrims, botanists, historians, or walkers enjoying the South Loch Ness Trail, all are welcome here to take a Fraser dram from the bottle which is never empty but never seen to be filled.

**Frisky** *adj.* (Scots) Someone who is staggering from drink.

**Fuzzle** *n.* (Scots) An alcoholic beverage or tipple.

# G

**Gaelic, Gaidhlig** *n*. The native Celtic language of Scotland that provides the etymological root for the majority of famous distillery names known across the whisky world. During the 18th century Scots Gaelic was the language that brought the name ***Uisge Beatha***, water of life to the world. Previously the commonly used generic name for distilled raw spirit was the Latin ***Aqua Vitae***, as produced for centuries in alembics across Europe. But in Scotland the craft of making quality whisky evolved in the 17th century. In the Highlands, the spirit was produced in a distinctive way using peat fired stills, malted barley and oak casks. The superior and distinctive flavour of this Highland spirit became increasingly popular and made it a much sought after distillation, differentiated from aqua vitae by its Gaelic name uisge beatha.

Following the Glorious Revolution and the 1745 Jacobite rebellion, the Hanoverian government embarked on a campaign of Highland suppression. Following its decisive victory at Culloden in 1746, a brutal pogrom was waged against Jacobite-supporting Highlanders including the outlawing of Highland culture and oppression of the Gaelic language. A direct result of this was the superimposition of English phonetic rules on all Gaelic names in written records. This resulted in the true Gaelic meanings of names and words becoming obscured to favour of ease of English pronunciation.

One single consequence was the conflation of the Gaelic words, *uisge beatha*, through Anglicised iterations of *usqeba, usquebae, usquebagh, usquabae, usquebey, usquibue, ushka, whiska* and finally the officially recognised confection *whisky*. The spelling of whisky as the generic name is particularly ironic for etymologists because the

Gaelic alphabet has no *w*, *k* or *y* and so the only surviving letters from uisge beatha are *h*, *i* and *s*.

**Gallon** *n*. (Scots) A Scottish traditional liquid measure equivalent in quantity to nearly three Imperial gallons.

**Gantress** *v*. To set or load barrels up onto a wooden gantress.
   *n*. The wooden stand specifically designed and shaped for supporting casks or barrels.

**Gardevin** *n*. (Scots) A big-bellied or square whisky jar or bottle holding around two quarts. A case, closet or cellaret for storing or transporting wine bottles, decanters etc.

**Gauger** (also **Gadger** or Scots Gaelic *Gàidsear*) *n*. (Scots) Derived from the duty of reading the 'gauges'. From the late 17th century, the common name given to any Customs and Excise Officer. Posted to every parish in Scotland, the gauger was charged with protecting the government's financial interest in whisky distilling by monitoring all production on legal distillery sites and any illegal goings-on in the area. This duty included setting out on search exercises to find and confiscate any illegal stills in the locality. Also to arrest and bring 'whisky smugglers' to justice to ensure all whisky produced paid the due tax. In the 18th and 19th centuries gaugers had difficulties living in remote rural communities where a compromise of duty and personal safety often had to be negotiated. Though modern technology means that HM Customs and Excise Officers are now centralised in data centres, the ghost of the gauger lives on, even if only in the computer systems. Now the gauger stalks the IT systems of distilleries, keeping a close eye on production volumes and HM government's grip on its duty.

**Gaw** *n*. (Scots) The head, or foreshots, of the still run. The first runnings of the spirit. Example of usage: *The gaw o' the pot.*

**Geosmin** *n.* The organic compound responsible for a musty or earthy taste or odour. This can sometimes be present as an off-odour in whisky that has become fouled in the cask or when the distillation has included damp cereal affected by bacterial growth. It is also the cause of the earthy 'petrichor' smell that arises and hangs in the air after rainfall.

**Germination** *n.* The first step in the malting process where dried barley grains are tricked into believing that spring has sprung by the introduction of warmth and water. In maltings, large batches of between thirty and fifty tonnes of barley are subjected to two days of steeping, drying and resting. Over three days the series of soaking and resting stages 'wakes' the barley and triggers the enzymes which access the starch stored in the grain kernel. The grain now produces cuilms, the tiny shoots and roots it puts out as necessary for regrowth. Historically, each distillery produced its own green malt in malting barns, but nowadays a few large malting specialists operating on a huge scale supply most of the industry's demand.

**Germination Kilning Vessel** – see **GKV**

**Gill** *v.* (Scots) To drink, to stop work for a tipple. A practice tradition- ally associated with trades and craftsmen who would break during the working day at noon for a gill or two.

    *n.* A liquid measure. One imperial gill is equal to 142 ml. The smaller Scots gill is ¾ of the imperial measure and ¼ of a mutchkin.

**Gill-bells** *n.* (Scots) The daily chiming of St Giles Cathedral's bells at 11.30 am. In 18th century Edinburgh these bells were known as the *Gill-bells* as they marked the signal to all working citizenry that it was time to down their tools and hurry along to their nearest howff or tavern. There they would partake of their **meridian** or midday chosen dram, a gill of whisky, brandy, or a tassie of ale or porter.

**Gillie**

**Gillie** *n*. (Scots) A gill of whisky.

**Gill-stoup** *n*. (Scots) A drinking vessel or pitcher holding a gill. Immortalised in the traditional 19th century Scots street ballad, 'Weary o' the Gill-stoup', beginning

> What mighty feats has whisky done,
> Its made some men stark naked run
> And wae their nose to shool the ground.
> As they were walking hame,
>
> O weary o the gill-stoup,
> the gill-stoup, the gill stoup
> O wae betide the gill-stoup,
> it breeds muckle grief at hame'.

**Gilp** *v*. (Scots) To spurt, spill, dash or splash into a glass. *n*. A small splash of water.

**Gird** *v*. (Scots) The act of encircling wooden barrel staves and sealing a cask with a metal hoop.
   *n*. Traditionally, a hoop of metal or wood crafted for a barrel or tub. In coopering the metal hoop is hammered down around the barrel by the cooper to fasten the staves together and seal the oak wood cask.

**Girtle** *v. and n.*(Scots) To spurt, spill, dash or splash into a glass. A small splash of water.

**Girvan** – see **Grain distilleries**

**Gizen** *adj*. (Scots) Of cask wood, dried out. Also of crops, desiccated. Also a person who is parched or thirsty.

**GKV** *n.* Acronym for Germination Kilning Vessel - massive circular stainless steel vats which are the multi-functioning vessels at the heart of the giant industrial maltster plants. The GKV is where the low moisture dried barley grains are transformed by steeping, germination and kilning into malted barley, ready for delivery to distilleries. A typical GKV will have the capacity to process between 100-350 tonnes of malt at one time. The design incorporates perforated, rotating steel floors and internal combs of ribbon turners which sift the barley grains malt. Malting in GKVs takes place over four to six days through the continuous supply and drainage of water, temperature controlled air venting and, where required, the introduction of peat smoke. The design of the chambers ensures that the maltsters can soak and dry vast quantities whilst ensuring consistent measurement and control of the moisture content to the levels required for storage and transport.

**Glag** (also **Glug, Glog**) *v.* (Scots) To drink making a loud audible glottal noise in the throat while swallowing.

**Glaggy** (also **Claggy**) *adj.* (Scots) Soft and sticky, used to describe a malt mash gone to thick sugary state.

**Glammie** *n.* (Scots) A mouthful of spirit.

**Glamp** *v.* (Scots) To gulp a mouthful of spirit down in one swallow.

**Glass-breaker** *n.* (Scots) A serious tippler or hard drinker.

**Gleann, Glen** *n.* (Scots Gaelic) Classically, a clefted hill or mountain landscape where water supply is abundant, shelter from severe weather is afforded by the surrounding hills, and crops and livestock can be nurtured on the nutrient-rich lower slopes. The Gaelic naming of a glen tends to focus on its unique physical, emotional and elemental landscape characteristics. This tradition also lends itself appositely to the naming of an individually crafted whisky. Glen is the most common and popular word to be found across the labels and in the naming of whisky brands, whether they be single malt or blends. In whisky making the particular 'glen' of production takes on the same significance as the **terroir** in French winemaking. In English the nearest equivalent is valley. Historically, the ubiquity of the *Glen-* prefix in whisky names reflects the natural choice of location for so many distilleries to be found in the heart of the Highland landscape.

**Glen Turret** *n.* Scotland's oldest working distillery. It began producing whisky in 1775 and is now home to the Famous Grouse Experience.

**Gless** *v.* (Scots) To drink a glass of spirits to the finish.

**Glibly** *adv.* (Scots) To swallow a spirit smoothly, quietly and easily.

**Glock** (also **Gluck**) *v.* (Scots) To gulp, gurgle. To pour through an opening that is too narrow and causes a reflux.

**Glossings** *n. pl.* (Scots) Rosy flushings on the face brought on by drinking alcohol.

**Glugger** (also **Gluther**) *v.* (Scots) To swallow greedily and noisily making a gurgling noise in the throat.

**Glycine** *n.* Glycine is one of the group of amino acids which includes **alanine**, **phenylalanine**, **tryptophan** and **tyrosine**. These are slowly absorbed in the fermentation of wort sugars then synthesised and absorbed by the yeast as it reaches the next generation bud stages of fermentation.

**Goldie** *n.* (Scots) The affectionate name for a nice, satisfying measure of whisky in an appropriate glass, usually prefaced by *a wee*. A dram.

**Gordon and MacPhail** *n.* Founded in 1895 in the Moray town of Elgin by James Gordon and John Alexander MacPhail, Gordon and MacPhail are one of the classic Highland whisky family businesses. Pioneers of the popularity of single malt whisky, the business opened in a handsome and ornate corner site as a 'family grocer, tea, wine and spirit merchants'. The firm showed great entrepreneurial instinct from early on as whisky merchants, particularly in selecting and brokering malt whisky. Location helped, situated amidst many well established and esteemed distilleries around Moray and Strathspey including Macallan, Glenlivet, Glen Grant, Linkwood and Mortlach. Soon the firm developed a reputation for bottling fine whisky by personally selecting casks from these distilleries and providing customers with a guarantee of quality whisky under the Gordon and MacPhail label.

The whisky brokering side of the business flourished in the 20th century under John Urquhart, who, having joined as a 15-year-old apprentice was made Senior Partner in the firm in 1915. Urquhart specialised in selecting and maturing single malt whiskies in his preferred Spanish, ex-sherry casks for longer and longer periods. At this time, few distilleries chose to bottle their whisky as single malt, preferring to supply it in bulk for the dominant global demand for mixing in the big selling blend brands. By 1950 Gordon and MacPhail held the largest range of bottled single malt whiskies in the world. However, the passion for malt whisky was yet to register in Scotland and in the 1960s the firm launched its 'Connoisseur's Choice' range of single malts from different distilleries in the rapidly expanding Italian, French, American and Dutch markets. The move was a success and triggered a wave of passion and interest in malt whisky which continues to flourish on the continent today. The Urquhart family connection continues, and Richard Urquhart and twin brother Stuart are the fourth generation of the family to guide Gordon and MacPhail's innovative approach to malt whisky marketing.

**Govellin** *adj.* (Scots) Staring mindlessly, as if drunk. Hanging loosely and ungracefully. Having the appearance of intoxicated eyes.

**Grain distilleries** *n.* Grain whisky distilleries are distinguished from malt distilleries in that they produce whisky using the twin column **Patent** or **Coffey** distilling method. By these means all stages of the production process take place within a continuous flow through the analyser and rectifier columns. Scotland currently has seven grain distilleries with a combined production of around 290 million litres of alcohol per year from vast quantities of maize, wheat and unmalted barley grains. This huge output mainly supplies grain whisky demand for making blended whisky.

- **Cameronbridge** by the river Leven in Fife is Scotland's oldest grain distillery, founded in 1824, and the largest, producing 100 million litres of alcohol per year (LAPA). It also produces its own famous single grain bottling, 'Cameron Brig'.
- **North British** (NB) opened in 1887. Today the NB is Scotland's second oldest and second biggest grain distillery, producing 64 million LAPA. In 2015 it celebrated producing its historic 2.5 billionth cask.
- French-owned **Starlaw** near Bathgate in West Lothian is Scotland's newest grain distillery, opening as recently as 2010 with a production capacity of around 25 million LAPA. It mainly supplies popular French brands 'Glen Turner' and 'Label 5', one of the world's top-selling blends owned by parent company La Martiniquaise.
- **Girvan** on the west coast was built by the Glenfiddich and Balvenie owning Grant family and opened in 1963, producing around 15 million LAPA.

- Located in Glasgow's historic Gorbals district the **Strathclyde** distillery was founded in 1927. Despite being geographically a Lowland distillery and its proximity to the river Clyde, Strathclyde's water supply comes directly from the celebrated Loch Ceiteirein/Katrine in the Trossachs at the Highland line boundary to the north of Glasgow. Such is the allure and beauty of the loch that it inspired Sir Walter Scott to write *The Lady of the Lake*.
- West of the Trossachs, on the other side of Ben Lomond, lies the **Loch Lomond Distillery**. Established at Alexandria in 1993, the distillery produces around 18 million LAPA.
- Located on the north shore of the Cromarty Firth, **Invergordon** is the most northernly grain distillery. Built in 1960 and now owned by Whyte and Mackay, Invergordon sources its water from Loch Glass high in the Ben Wyvis massif and produces around 40 million LAPA including its own Invergordon label aged single grain bottlings.

**Grain whisky** *n*. Whilst malt whisky is made exclusively in batches using malted grains of barley, grain whisky is produced in the continuous industrial **Coffey** or **Patent** still using cereal grains such as wheat and maize and smaller amounts of unmalted barley. As with malt whisky production the process is entirely natural, using just heat, water, yeast and the cereal grains. In terms of efficiency the output from a grain distillery can be more than ten times that of an average sized malt distillery. Most grain whisky is used as the basic volume spirit for blended whisky, being mixed with carefully selected and distinctive malt whiskies. As with malt, grain whisky is matured in oak casks for at least three years. However, the continuous distillation produces a lighter flavoured spirit than the pot distilled malt whisky. Grain whisky takes longer than malt whisky to take on any deeper distinctive flavour characteristics. In the glass, grain whisky is often described as being flat and feinty, being less weighty and lacking the depth and layered complexity of a malt finish. This largely reflects the lack of time and effort spent on maturing grain whisky as demand is for blend-ready bulk spirit whisky. Some distilleries do mature, bottle and sell their own branded single grain whisky, or blend grain whiskies from other distilleries, to create a blended grain. These single grain brands are well respected and have been nurtured over the years to show all the complexity and quality of a good malt in the glass.

**Gray-pig** (also **Grey-beard**) *n*. (Scots) A ceramic whisky jar.

**Green Malt** *n*. Green malt is barley which has been soaked to stimulate germination, producing shoots and roots (or **cuilms**) and heated to trigger germination. These vibrant growing grains may have a moisture content as high as 48%. The green malt phase also triggers the production of starch in the kernel. This transient stage is stalled by dehydrating the barley grains through hot air or kilning to bring the moisture content down to the required 4.5%. This stops full germination into the plant stage whilst maintaining the starches and energy within the malt for the next stage in the mashtun.

**Greetin-fu'** *adj*. (Scots) Someone who is at the maudlin, emotional, tearful stage of drunkenness.

**Grist** *n*. When the barley grains are cracked open in the malt mills they release the white powdery starch from the husk. The crushed malt is now grist, to be conveyed to the grist hopper in readiness for mashing. Grist that is too coarse produces less fermentable material and therefore less alcohol yield. Too fine a grist causes sludging in the mash that is difficult to drain and loss of overall alcohol yield. Experienced maltmen can tell by the **maltman's rub**, between thumb and forefinger, whether the grist is of the right consistency. A more scientific test is to pass the grist through two sieves which separates it into three parts. Good grist for a traditional mash tun should consist of around 70% **grits**, 20% **husk**, and 10% flour.

**Grister** *n.* (Scots) One who delivers the grist into the mill.

**Grits** *n.* In the malt mill stage barley kernels are broken into husks, grits and flour. The grits are the small pieces of the crushed core grain. Grits are widely used outwith distilling and sold separately as a healthy food ingredient in supermarkets or health food stores. Barley grits can be consumed as a hot cereal. In the southern United States they are a traditional base ingredient for some savoury dishes.

**Gruse** *n.* (Scots) Sediment, grinds.

**Gully bottle** *n.* (Scots) A big-bellied whisky bottle.

**Gunn, Neil** *n.* Like Robert Burns before him, Neil Gunn (1891-1973) was a writer who wrestled with his role as an Excise Officer while also feeling a strong connection to the land, the people and the past. Highlander Gunn's existential questioning of this relationship with the natural world shines through in his writings. This is from his 1944 novel *The Green Isle of the Great Deep*, on the making of whisky:

'A wise man will give the best he can distil with the finest grace, when he gives freely and without reward.'

**Gust-fu** *adj.* (Scots) Full of relish, palatable, enjoyable in the mouth.

**Gusty** *adj.* (Scots) Satisfying, tasty. Pleasing on the palate.

**Gyle-fat** *n.* (Scots) The vat or vessel used for fermenting the wort.

**Gyle house** *n.* (Scots) A brew house.

**Gysen** *adj.* (Scots) Dried out. Used in the context of the wood of a barrel that is parched, warped and leaky.

# H

**Hairst** (also **Hearst**) *v*. To harvest or gather in from the fields.
    *n*. (Scots) The harvest.

**Half-moon flask** *n*. A large transport flask specially designed for smuggling. The shape of the flask is designed in such a way as to be worn on the body, almost encircling the smuggler but invisible to an untrained eye.

**Half-mutchkin** *n*. (Scots) A measure of liquid equivalent to two gills, or an eighth of a Scots pint or Joug amounting to around 0.10 of a litre.

**Half-on** (also **Hauf-on, Half-sea and Hauf-sea**) *adj*. (Scots) Well on the way to drunkenness. Tipsy, drunk.

**Hammer Mill** *n*. A powerful and effective crushing mill which uses small percussive hammers to break open grains and render them the optimum size for mashing. Hammer mills are generally used in the production of grist from maize and wheat for grain whisky production. In malt whisky production, the roller mill method is preferred. It offers a more exact and precise control of the gap between the milling rollers and measurement of the pressure on the grains thus enabling the master to select the size and composition of the malt grist.

**Hans in kelder!** *excl*. (Scots) A family toast drunk to the health of an unborn infant and the mother carrying it.

# Hash

**Hash** *v*. (Scots) To work at speed and under pressure. A word traditionally associated with Strathspey and the maltmen in the malting barns turning mounds of heavy malting barley using wooden shiels (paddles). Before mechanical ploughs were introduced, this repetitive job required manual speed and effort to ensure even turning and drying. After years in the malt barn, the maltmen would often develop a repetitive strain injury which came to be known as '**Monkey Shoulder**'.

**Head** *n*. In the second distillation in the spirit or low wines still, the spirit run is separated into three component fractions. These are the **head**, **heart**, and **tail**, also known as the **foreshots**, **middle cut** and the **feints**. The first fifteen to thirty minutes of the run from the spirit still is too pungent as it contains heavy oils and esters which have attached to the copper surface of the still and condenser from the previous distillation. The head is therefore unusable as spirit with a high ABV of around 85% and contains a high proportion of volatile flavour-influencing compounds and sulphides visible in the spirit still in the verdigris colouration. The head is run off to the feints receiver and used to start the next batch.

**Heart** *n*. At the second distillation stage the *heart* is the desired premium spirit in the run, comprising the finest fraction of the batch to be sent to the spirit receiver and thereafter to mature in the oak casks and become Scotch whisky. At the start of its run the heart is 72-75% ABV. As the run progresses the alcohol strength and quality falls away until the stillman deems them to be **tails** or **feints** and they are diverted to the low wines and feints receiver for recycling or disposal. The volume of heart collected varies from distillery to distillery but will be in the range of 15-20% of the low wines and feints charge. The head and tails or foreshots and feints are combined and recycled in the next batch. The still operator decides when to make the cut and change from heart to feints, usually at the stage when alcohol strength is in the range 57-64% ABV. Each distillery differs and the decision as to when to make the cut is another signature factor in creating the distinct flavour characteristics of individual whiskies.

**Heat Exchanger** *n.* Heat exchangers are simple but effective piping systems which save energy by transferring heat between hot and cold fluids passing against each other. In distilleries, they are used to recycle the heat from the hot, processed liquids to the cold, fresh liquids and vice versa. As the freshly fermented wash from the washbacks is pumped through to the wash charger in the still-room it passes through a heat exchanger. Here it meets hot, spent wash from the previous still run which can be as high as 100°C. This brings the fresh wash up to still temperature by simple heat exchange, saving energy by preheating the next wash charge as it runs into the still.

**Hemicellulose** *n.* A major source of flavour components occur-ring in oak wood. Hemicellulose contains a rich variety of sugars, xylose, mannose, galactose, rhamnose, arabinose and glucose and breaks down easily when heated in charring or flaming of oak casks. These sugars become accessible as the spirit penetrates the wood, contributing significantly to the aroma compounds estab-lishing in the spirit during maturation. The flavour compounds it triggers are furfural which delivers almond, walnut and grainy flavour notes; hydroxymethylfurfural, producing musty, waxy, caramel and butter notes; cyclotene delivering rich caramel, maple and liquorice; and maltol which produces sweet and malty tones.

**Her Majesty's Revenue and Customs** *n.* Her Majesty's Revenue and Customs (HMRC) is the enforcement authority for the verification of Scotch whisky, charged with ensuring that the government collects its appropriate Tax take of Excise

Duty and VAT from each bottle of whisky. HMRC officers are actively responsible for ensuring the compliance of Scotch whisky producers with the Scotch Whisky Regulations in all areas of production, labelling and marketing. The level of tax levied on Scotch whisky is a perennial issue to be argued over by the lobbying Scotch Whisky producers and HM Treasury. Tax on a bottle of Scotch Whisky currently stands at 76% of retail price which means around £16 of every £20 average bottle of Scotch whisky goes to the UK Treasury.

**Het pint** (also **Het stoup**) *n.* (Scots) A drink composed of whisky and ale drunk on Hogmanay, on the night preceding a marriage or in celebration of a child's birth.

**Heuch!** *excl.* (Scots) The exuberant exclamation expressed in celebration of participation in a wild, spirited Highland dance such as 'Strip the Willow' or 'Dashing White Sergeant'. An exclamation of excitement or exhilaration. The cry is usually uttered by the male dancers to celebrate successfully accomplishing a highly technical point of the dance at speed.

**Hielan' Blue** *n.* (Scots) A generic name for any peated Highland whisky.

**Highland** *n. and adj.* One of the five protected regions of Scotch Whisky production, Highland is defined as lying north of The Highland Line. The region also includes the whisky producing islands of Arran, Harris, Jura, Lewis, Mull, Orkney, Raasay and Skye. Highland whiskies are characteristically spicy, fruity and full flavoured.

**Highland line** *n.* The defined boundary of that part of Scotland characterised as producing 'Highland' whisky. In the year following the great famine of 1783, the Wash Act was introduced to alleviate hardship in the Highland counties. These were defined as the counties of Orkney, Caithness, Sutherland, Ross, Inverness, Argyll, Bute, Stirling, Lanark, Perth, Dumbarton, Aberdeen, Forfar, Kincardine, Banff, Nairn and Moray. Today in the Scotch Whisky Regulations the boundary itself is described as 'the line beginning at the North Channel and running along the southern foreshore of the Firth of Clyde to Greenock, and from there to Cardross Station, then eastwards in a straight line to the summit of Earl's Seat in the Campsie Fells, and then eastwards in a straight line to the Wallace Monument, and from there eastwards along the line of the B998 and A91 roads until the A91 meets the M90 road at Milnathort, and then along the M90 northwards until the Bridge of Earn, and then along the River Earn until its confluence with the River Tay, and then along the southern foreshore of that river and the Firth of Tay until it comes to the North Sea.'

**High wines** *n.* Another name for the spirit or second distillate collected from the second or low wines still. A name more commonly associated with the production of Bourbon whiskey than Scotch whisky. In that production process, high wines are the finished spirit to be filled into new charred, white oak casks.

**Histidine** *n.* One of the slower acting amino acids absorbed at the early stage of the malted barley fermentation process in the washback. It feeds and expands on the sugar in the wort together with the slower amino acids **Isoleucine**, **Leucine**, **Methionine** and **Valine**.

**Hogget** (also **Hogshead** or **Hogsheid**) *n.* (Scots). A large cask or barrel containing around 250 litres of liquor. One of the standard sizes of casks selected for filling and finishing the spirit. Made from either American or European oak, the sherry hogget is similar in shape and around half the size of the sherry butt. Coopers can create Dump hogsheads from smaller 200 litre bourbon barrels by increasing the number of staves in a bourbon barrel to give the same capacity.

**Hogmanay** *n*. (Scots) The Scots celebration of the turn of the year into the New Year. There is no better explanation of the tradition than this 1847 definition from the Dictionary of the Scottish Language:

> 'It is still customary, in retired and primitive towns, for the children of the poorer class of people to get themselves on that morning swaddled in a great sheet, doubled up in front, so as to form a vast pocket, and then go along the streets in little bands, calling at the doors of the wealthier classes for an expected dole of oaten bread. Each child gets one quadrant section of oat-cake (sometimes, in the case of particular favourites, improved by an addition of cheese), and this is called their Hogmanay. The children, on coming to the door, cry: "Hogmanay! ... Get up, goodwife, and shake your feathers and dinna think that we are beggars. For we are bairns come out to play, get up and gie's our hogmanay!"'

**Hooch** *n*. A slang name used to describe any alcohol illicitly distilled in the British Isles or North America. Generally non-matured and clear spirit with a very high Alcohol by Volume (ABV) content but no particular character or brand identity.

**Hooker** *n*. (Scots) A generous glass of whisky. A goodly dram.

**Hooter** *n*. (Scots) A very large whisky. A bumper dram.

**Horn** *n*. (Scots) A traditional drinking vessel created from the horn of a ram. A draught of liquor.

**Horn–dry** *adj*. (Scots) Thirsty. Craving for a drink.

**Horning** *n.* (Scots) A satisfactory supply of alcoholic drink.

**Howff** *n.* (Scots) Any drinking establishment. An inn. A small public house that is informally kept but dependably open for its customers.

**Hummy** *adj.* (Scots) Ale or liquor that is strong, heady and foamy.

**Husk** *n.* The papery outer shell of the barley grain which becomes detached during the milling. Following milling the grist that goes into a traditional mash tun consists of a mix of around 70% grits, 20% husk and 10% flour. At the end of the mashing the filtered out husk matter remains in the mashtun in the draff residue for recycling as cattle feed.

**Hydroxyproline** *n.* In fermentation hydroxyproline is one of the slowest absorbed amino acids at the end of the fermentation cycle. Its presence is apparent as the yeast exhausts the sugars in the wort and approaches the end of its growth potential.

# I

**Illicit Distillation (Scotland) Act 1822** *n.* In 1822 the United Kingdom government's patience snapped over the ineffectiveness of its measures to stamp out illicit distilling and Justices of the Peace had their discretionary power to reduce penalties removed. The Illicit Distillation (Scotland) Act set high mandatory financial penalties of £200 for those found guilty of possessing un-gauged stills, operating unlicensed stills or smuggling unlicensed whisky. The owners of any property where illicit distilling took place were liable for fines up to £100. Furthermore, the Excise Officers could destroy illicit stills, wash and spirit without a warrant from the Justice of the Peace. Under this tough new regime 6,278 cases were tried in 1822 relating to illicit distilling.

**Illicit distilling** *n.* By the mid-17th century, small scale distilling was widespread across Scotland but the government realised there was substantial income to be gathered from the legalisation and taxing of spirit production. The result was the 1664 Excise Act which placed a new tax of two shillings and eight pence *'to be levied on every pint produced of aqua vitae'*, the first of many such Acts of Parliament. However, it also kickstarted a new era of whisky smuggling, as small distillers devised methods of tax avoidances including operating in hidden locations using mobile pot stills of twenty-five to forty gallons. In response, a crown enforcement service was created with Government officers charged to chase down all illegal distilling, storage and marketing of whisky. Out in the country a new bogeyman appeared to stalk the hills, glens and coastlines of Scotland: *The Exciseman*.

# Immature Spirits (Restrictions) Act 1915

Despite their best efforts illicit distilling flourished, especially in the Highlands, with growing demand for the quality whisky produced in the area. In an era of cat and mouse manoeuvring there are many recorded incidents of violent clashes and even gunfire between the Excise officers and smugglers. The government's hand was often thwarted legally by the unwillingness of the Justices of the Peace, usually the local landlord, to impose any weight of punishment since in most cases the distiller was also a tenant and supplier of fine whisky to the same landlord.

**Immature Spirits (Restrictions) Act 1915** *n.* In 1915 the Immature Spirits (Restriction) Act was a prohibition-driven piece of British legislation. The Act was brought in during World War I in response to demands that grain production for the making of alcohol be prohibited during wartime. Its origins lay in the passionate campaigning of the teetotal politician David Lloyd George, whose aim was to put the alcoholic spirit industry, especially whisky, out of business. In the first twelve months of the war the British Parliament debated why the country's armaments production was failing to meet its targets and, in a famous speech at Bangor, Lloyd George pointed the finger at the alcohol trade: 'Drink is doing more damage in the war than all the German submarines put together'.

This coincided with a public and political campaign against the widespread availability of the cheap, immature whisky that was held responsible for widespread social problems. Among Lloyd George's proposals were a policy of prohibition, and the establishment of a Central Control Board to restrict pub opening hours and ban the purchase of 'rounds'. A measure aimed directly at the whisky industry in the 1915 Budget was the proposal to double the duty on spirits, which caused outrage and opposition from Scottish and Irish MPs.

James Stevenson, of Kilmarnock's John Walker & Sons, posited the introduction of compulsory bonding for a period of two years to establish a quality threshold and remove cheap immature spirits from the market.

Facing defeat on his Budget, Lloyd George dropped the duty proposal but adopted Stevenson's new bonding rule. The **Immature Spirits (Restriction) Act 1915 legislated for the first time that the alcohol must be matured in oak casks for a minimum of two years, extended to three years in 1916**. This measure elevated whisky's status and ensured that the quality of Scotch was significantly improved, thus enshrining in legislation one of the key principles of Scotch whisky: **that all spirit must be matured for three years in a bonded ware-house before it can be sold as Scotch whisky**.

**India** *n*. India is among the top ten export markets for Scotch whisky, importing over 40 million litres each year. It also maintains one of the world's oldest continuous whisky distilling traditions. Scotch whisky was introduced or exported to India in the early 19th century during the British Raj. The first production was in the 1820s when Englishman Edward Dyer set about building a brewery and distillery in the Himalayan hill settlement of Kasauli. Dyer brought all the equipment he needed from England and Scotland, transporting it by boat up the Ganges and thereafter ascending 1900 metres on ox carts to build the world's highest malt whisky distillery. Dyer was passionate about creating fine malt whisky and chose the location due to the similarity of the hill climate to Scotland and the ready availability of fresh spring water.

The Kasauli distillery is still operating today and is one of the oldest continuously operating whisky distilleries in the world, still using some of the original plant and copper stills. Dyer's malt whisky distillery is an exception however, as most Indian whisky production is more akin to rum distilling, using the fermented sugars in molasses rather than malted grains. Any malt whisky distilled in India is not aged significantly and tends to be added to the molasses whisky to give a more authentic whisky flavour.

**Indrink**

Amrut Distilleries bottled and launched the first Indian pure single malt in 2004. Despite its long relationship with whisky and links to Scotland, India has developed a unique approach to authentic Scotch Whisky. To restrict the growth of imported Scotch Whisky's market share it applies tariffs of up to 150%, successfully restricting market penetration to just 1%.

**Indrink** *v. and n.* (Scots) To evaporate. To shrink in, become less. Evaporation, shrinkage or diminution of stored liquid, loss of liquid quantity in storage.

**Ingle** *n.* (Scots) Furnace of the kiln. A fireplace or hearth. A flame. A burning peat, coal or log. A faggot or bundle of fuel.

**Ingle-gleed** *n.* (Scots) The blazing glow of the kiln fire.

**Inland Revenue** *n.* The government body established in the 17th century, to levy and collect taxes to pay for its foreign adventures, is best known for its annual campaign to ensure all individuals report and pay the appropriate level of Income Tax. In the past, it has levied taxes on such diverse products as newspapers, hats, gloves, hair powder, land, playing cards and of course, whisky!

**Interactive maturation** *n.* The combination and interaction of all the ingredients and the processes within the distillery in the production of the spirit. Individual elements are: the location of the distillery, type of barley, malting process, origin and quantity of peat, strain of yeast, copper still shapes, water sources and the temperature regimes applied throughout the production process. All play their part in adding character to the spirit batch as it processes towards filling the cask. Thereafter, the warehouse construction and location, mean air temperature and humidity continue to influence the flavours as the cask lies in the warehouse for a minimum of three years. During this part of the process the whisky's character is established through this interactive maturation and the distinctive terroir characteristics of each distillery.

**Invergordon** – see **Grain distilleries**

**Ireland** *n.* In Ireland whiskey tends to be triple distilled as opposed to the two still approach in Scotland. Ireland can claim an earlier written reference to production of *aqua vitae* than Scotland. It occurs in 1405 in the *'Annals of Clonmacnoise'* where it is recorded that the *Chieftain of the Moyntyreolas, Richard Magranell*, died at Christmas from *'taking a surfeit of aqua vitae.'* As with Scotland, the art of distilling was almost certainly introduced by monks who had learned their craft on the continent. But the medicinal use and benefits of *aqua vitae* were soon eclipsed by recreational consumption which brought the attention of the government and the Crown. Finally, in 1608 King James I granted the first licence to landowner Sir Thomas Phillips of Bushmills, County Antrim, which now lays claim as the oldest continuously working licensed distillery in the world, although the current distillery dates only from 1784.

By 1779 it was reckoned that there were 1,228 working distilleries from which only a fraction of proper duty was collected. Following aggressive legislation to collect tax revenues, licence all distillers and raise the cost of operating distilleries, the number was reduced to just 32 licensed distilleries by 1821. That said, the production of illicit *poteen* in the north west remained rampant in the poorer agricultural areas where it was a tradeable commodity between tenant farmers and landowners. Currently there are around 16 distilleries operating in Ireland and about 800 people employed in production and marketing. Ireland is also ironically the birthplace of Scotland's massive grain whisky production capacity thanks to Aeneas Coffey who took the basic continuous still process developed by Scotsman Robert Stein in 1827 and turned it into a vertical column model which is still used on an industrial scale today across Scotland's seven grain whisky distilleries.

**Irish Spirit** *n*. Besides Irish whiskey, the most famous Irish spirit in continuous production is the pot still produced *poitín*. Traditionally produced in the north and west in small, poor agricultural areas on tenant farms as a trading product of the land. Produced in small batches, informally and well away from the scrutiny of officialdom, the decision to run a still is often down to intelligence about the presence of the *Gardaí* in the area. Further counter measures are traditionally taken by setting a still on disputed land boundaries to confuse the identity of the owner. In Scotland, illicit mountain stills were fired by juniper bushes for the whiter, invisible smoke they produced. In Ireland peat or turf was used to fire the still and, since the aromatic smoke was a dead giveaway, stills could only be run on days when the weather was grey and windy enough to disperse it. The tradition continues today without the worries of smoke since bottled gas is freely available.

**Irish Whiskey** *n*. Irish whiskey is generally produced using a triple distillation process and must be distilled and matured in Ireland. Like Scotch whisky, Irish whiskey is a protected global brand and defined by strict regulations. These are: that it must be distilled on the island of Ireland including the Republic of Ireland and Northern Ireland; it must be produced from a mash of malted cereals with or without whole grains of other cereals; and the mash must have been saccharified by the diastase of malt contained within the grain, with or without other natural enzymes. It must be fermented by the action of yeast, then distilled at an alcoholic strength of less than 94.8% ABV.

Like Scotch it is subject to the maturation of the final distillate for at least three years in wooden casks such as oak, not exceeding 700 litres (185 US gallons and 154 imperial gallons) capacity. Maturation can only take place on the island of Ireland. Caramel colouring (E150a) may be added. At bottling Irish whiskey must have a minimum alcohol by volume content of 40%. There are specifications for three varieties of Irish whiskey: Single Pot Still, Single Malt and Blended whiskey. Irish whiskey is a protected European Geographical Indication (GI) product and the production, labelling and marketing of Irish whiskey must be verified by the Irish revenue authorities as conforming with the Department of Agriculture's file for Irish whiskey.

**Iskie-bae** *n.* (Scots) A regional Scots pronunciation for whisky based on the Gaelic *Uisge beatha.*

**Island** *adj.* A distinct and growing category of whiskies produced in traditional and non-traditional island locations. Once exclusively the domains of Islay, Jura, Mull, Orkney and Skye, this category has expanded in the last two decades and now includes Arran, Harris, Lewis and Raasay with plans progressing for distilleries on Shetland and Tiree.

**Islay** *n.* (From Scots Gaelic *Isla*) The Isle of Islay in Argyll is one of Scotland's protected regions of whisky production. Islay's whiskies are recognised as the most distinctive of all Scotland's single malts for their characteristic smoky, phenolic flavour notes of peat, TCP, brine, and seaweed. With eight working distilleries currently producing distinctively different whiskies, and its own on-island maltings at **Port Ellen**, Islay is uniquely popular as a 'whisky tourism' destination. Each year it draws groups from all over the world who criss-cross the island ticking off Islay's whisky areas and the distilleries in each. On the north-east coast sit **Caol Ila** and **Bunahabhainn** (with a new distillery at **Ardnahoe** due to open in 2018). In the middle, around the shores of Loch Indaal, are **Bruichladddich**, 'sleeping' **Port Charlotte** and **Bowmore**. Out in the west on the Atlantic coast at **Kilchoman** lies Islay's youngest and Scotland's second most westerly distillery.

Fringing its south coast, the old peaty heavyweights of **Laphroaig**, **Lagavulin** and **Ardbeg** look out across the Sound of Jura to Kintyre.

Islay's journey to pre-eminence as one of the defined whisky regions has its roots in an historic public affray (or *rammy*) in Glasgow. In 1725 Daniel Campbell, Glasgow Shawfield MP from 1716-34, boldly voted in favour of a three pence *(3d)* per bushel Malt Tax on ale production. This caused uproar amongst the poorer groups of consumers, no more so than in Glasgow where Campbell's own constituents were so outraged that they targeted and ransacked his Shawlands mansion house in the infamous Shawfield riots. In recognition of the great criminal damage and loss he had suffered, according to his own inventory, the City of Glasgow awarded Campbell £9,000 in compensation.

He was already established as a prosperous merchant, ship owner and brandy black marketer trading with North America and the West Indies. Now the canny Campbell used the sum to fund the purchasing of the Isle of Islay and part of Jura in 1726 from his debtor John Campbell of Cawdor for just £12,000, and took on his great project of improving the economy of Islay and Jura. For the next 120 years, the Shawfield Campbells ruled Islay with benevolent impunity, introducing industrial and agricultural enterprises which laid the ground for the establishment of the island's whisky industry.

The last hereditary chieftain in the line was John Francis, Daniel's great-great-great- grandson, born in Edinburgh in 1821, and heir to a diminishing family fortune. A senior London civil servant by profession, John Francis never took up his entitlement as his father was forced to sell Islay to James Morrison of Berkshire, alias Baron Margadale, whose family still own a large part of the island. JF Campbell comforted himself instead by plunging into his celebrated life's work of recording his love of the Islay people and culture, the result being his *'Popular Tales of the West Highlands'* (1860-62).

**Isoleucine** *n*. One the slower group of amino acids absorbed at the early stage of the fermentation process. Together with histidine, leucine, methionine and valine it is among the first to be synthesised as the yeast in the washback feeds and expands on the sugar in the wort.

Juniper

# J

**Jack Daniel's** – see **Daniel**

**Jairblins** *n. pl.* (Scots) Drops of liquor dripped into a glass. Dregs or leftover liquor in any drinking vessel.

**Japan** *n.* Records of whisky distilling in Japan date from the late 1800s but, thanks to two enterprising Scotch Whisky pioneers, following their dreams in the 1920s, Japan is now the world's second largest producer of malt whisky with nine malt distilleries. The founding fathers of the Japanese Whisky industry are **Shinjuri Torii**, who established the country's first whisky distillery, and his distiller **Masataka Taketsuru**, who introduced Scottish distilling expertise to create the country's first commercial whisky brand.

Torii was a chemist whose passion was for brewing and distilling. In his first foray into the drinks industry he created a Portuguese-style fortified wine, Akadama, which became very popular. Encouraged, he rose to the challenge of creating a Scotch style whisky, suited to Japan's climate, that would be embraced by the softer Japanese palate. Choosing the moist location of Yamazaki, between Osaka and Kyoto on Honshu island, he set up the Kotobukiya Company (which later became Suntory) and began building Japan's first malt whisky distillery in 1923.

A key to his eventual success was in hiring Masataka Taketsuru, whose family had owned a Sake brewery since 1733. Masataka returned from a sojourn to Scotland in 1918, where he had studied Organic Chemistry at the University of Glasgow before undertaking a distillery apprenticeship at Longmorn in Strathspey. After moving to Bo'ness he met and married a Scots girl, Jessie (Rita) Cowan of Kirkintilloch. The couple moved together to Campbeltown, where he completed his apprenticeship at Hazelburn. By 1920 Shinjiro Torii was searching for a distiller to take forward his whisky project and the return of Taketsuru with his Scots wife provided the basis for a partnership to launch Japanese 'Scotch' whisky.

Torii's Kotobukiya company soon evolved into the giant Suntory. In 1934 Masataka left to create his own distilling company, Nikka. He set about building the Yoichi distillery on the North island of Hokkaido on the shores of the Sea of Japan, surrounded by mountains on three sides, where he believed the 'terroir' was most similar in climate and landscape to Scotland. The devoted couple were parted when Rita died in 1961. In Yoichi, Rita Road commemorates her contribution to Japan's whisky history. Both Suntory and Nikka flourished and today are major international players who produce award-winning single malts comparable to those produced in Scotland. There are currently nine malt distilleries and five grain distilleries in operation, from Yoichi in the north to Yamazaki in the south. Japanese malts have been described as akin in character to Scotland's Lowlands and Speyside. However, there are some which use peated malt to create strong, smoky, phenolic expressions which are similar to Scotland's Islay brands. Japan's whisky industry maintains strong ties with Scotland's and there is great respect for the distinctive qualities of each Japanese distillery, and the growing recognition they achieve outside of Japan.

**Jaunty-bottle** (also **Jaunty-jug**) *n.* (Scots) A pocket whisky flask.

**Jeddart-jug** *n.* (Scots) A brass jug containing about eight gills used as a standard measure equivalent to around two pints or 1.13 litres. Also traditionally used as measure for dry goods such as flour and grain.

**Jeroboam** *n.* A large bottle, bowl or goblet with a capacity of around 4.5 litres for still wine.

**Jirble** (also **Jirgle**) *v.* (Scots) To shakily pour the liquid contents of a vessel so as to spill them, to empty a small quantity of liquid back and forth from one vessel to another, to pour unsteadily.

**Jirbling** *v.* (Scots) Spilling of liquor spots here and there.

**Jirblings** *n. pl.* (Scots) Dregs left in the bottom of a vessel when a single dram glass has been shared around a company

**Jock Tamson** *n.* (Scots) Colloquial Scots name for whisky.

**John Barleycorn** *n.* A traditional name for whisky. Celebrated in the many-versioned English folk song which narrates the journey of the barley corn through its transition from the field to the glass as if it were in the form of a man being pursued, captured, tortured and tormented in verses which mirror the stages of harvest, threshing, malting and brewing to produce the final liquor. In 1782 Scotland's National Bard, Robert Burns, published his own take on the tale which has become the template for most modern renditions. Burns sets the scene thus:

> There was three kings into the east,
> Three kings both great and high,
> And they hae sworn a solemn oath
> John Barleycorn should die.

**Johnny Maut** *n.* (Scots) Traditional name for malt liquor.

**Jug** *v.* (Scots) A measuring vessel kept by dispensers of liquor to serve up a Scots pint. The most famous example, regarded as setting the national standard measure for a pint, was the 'Jug of Stirling' or the 'pint stope of Stirling'. More generally the narrow spouted water vessel shaped to deliver a controlled measure of water to the spirit. Usually they are ceramic, glass or crystal, topped with a narrow beak to deliver a minimal droplet of water. Given their wide use in public houses, whisky jugs were soon recognised as a great opportunity for product placement and brand reinforcement by whisky producers. As a result, branded vintage whisky jugs are now highly collectible as an enthusiast's item and are brought out for whisky tastings.

*n.* To drink. To tipple. To neck. To measure liquor to the pint standard.

**Juggie** *n.* (Scots) A small vessel for drinking punch.

**Juit** (also **Jute**) *v.* (Scots) To tipple. To sip.
*n.* Tasteless or flat liquor. Any insipid or weak drink. Whisky dregs or sediment. Watery tea.

**Juniper** *n.* Though its natural spirit association is with gin, juniper also has a strong association with illicit whisky making. In the open landscape of the Highlands, a smoke trail was easily spotted by excise officers. Juniper therefore was the perfect fuel for firing illicit stills as it produces no visible smoke when burned.

**Jura** *n.* This small Hebridean island, thirty miles long and seven broad, with a population of just 200, is dwarfed in whisky terms by its neighbour Islay. Jura is famous as the remote retreat location chosen by George Orwell as he wrote his portentous novel *'1984'*. Ironically, 200 years prior to that date 'Big Brother' had already intervened oppressively in the lives of the *Diuraich* (Scots Gaelic name for Jura folk) in 1781. Then the Scottish parliament outlawed all small-scale distilling on the island, including for home consumption. The Craighouse distillery on the east side of the island opened in 1810 with a production capacity of 180,000 gallons per annum but fell silent in the late 1800s under James Ferguson and Sons who finally closed and dismantled it in 1901. It remained in a state of disrepair until two local estate owners joined forces to bring it back to life in 1963. Famous for its tall stills, the Jura distillery now produces a range of four whiskies ranging from sweet and unpeated to heavily peated.

**Justerini and Brooks** *n.* The unlikely names behind the world's second biggest selling Scotch whisky, J&B Rare. The firm was founded as Justerini and Johnson in 1749 by Giacomo Justerini of Bologna, who arrived in London in pursuit of the subject of his affections, opera singer Margherita Bellini. Whilst he failed in that romantic quest his new wine business succeeded, so well that he was able to sell it in 1760 and retire home to Italy. His founding partner George Johnson bought him out but kept Justerini's name on the brass plaque. The Brooks name was added when the business was sold on in 1830 to young, rich and well-connected George Brooks. So wealthy was Brooks that he was reputed to have a garden large enough for a snipe shoot at his St Johns Wood residence in London. His arrival triggered an era of growth for the firm as it built up an exclusive list of private clients and restaurants, including such stellar figures of the day as Charles Dickens.

As markets expanded both at home and abroad into the 20th century J&B became increasingly aware of the growing taste for blended Scotch whisky and began buying up select premier single malts for creating its own-brand house whiskies. J&B Rare was created specifically for the American market and launched in the USA in 1933 just as Prohibition ended. Sales of J&B Rare have grown ever since so that it is now the world's second largest selling Scotch whisky after Johnnie Walker with five Queen's Awards for Export Achievement. Today the firm advises on the cellars of Buckingham Palace, supplying clients from some of the best-known estates in France, Italy and Germany and is amongst the largest importers of domaine bottled Burgundy, Barolo and Riesling in the UK.

**Juttie** *n.* (Scots) A tippler.

The settlers came rolling in from

KentUcky

They found a new home in places like Buckie

# K

**Keechan** (also **Keechin**) *n.* (Scots) The liquor produced at the wash stage when the malt has been mashed and fermented and is ready to fill into the still for distillation.

**Keeve** *n.* (Scots) A large mashing vat or tub.

**Keisen** (Also **Keizen, Keasen**) *v.* (Scots) To dry out. To parch and shrink as in barley grains or wood.

**Keltie's mends** (also a **Kelty** or **Keltie**) *n.* (Scots) From Kelty in Fife. A bumper, or deliberately large dram, poured for a reluctant drinker. A *punishment* measure of whisky poured for a *softie,* that is someone who has rudely declined a host's offer.
    *adj.* Generous, Plentiful.

**Kentucky** *n.* It is estimated that as much as £200 million is spent annually overseas purchasing certain necessary foreign materials for making Scotch whisky in Scotland. Most of this cash gets banked in the eastern United States and more specifically in the State, or *Commonwealth* of Kentucky. This is because the Bluegrass state supplies around 90% of the twenty million oak casks quietly maturing and filled with whisky in warehouses around Scotland. Kentucky also produces 95% of the world's Bourbon whiskey. Just as Scotch whisky has strict defining laws as to where and how it must be produced, so similar rules apply to Bourbon. The spirit must be distilled from a grain mixture that is at least 51% corn, and aged in new, charredoak barrels. Furthermore, these requirements state that bourbon whisky for US consumption must be:

- distilled to no more than 80% ABV,
- filled into the barrel for ageing at no more than 62.5% ABV,
- bottled at minimum 40% ABV.

Since Bourbon barrels can only be used once, these previously used barrels are perfect first fill casks for Scotch whisky. For cost efficiency, these barrels are carefully dismantled, then flat packed for bulk shipping in containers across the Atlantic. In Scotland the Bourbon infused oak staves are reassembled in Scottish cooperages as hogsheads for filling with new make spirit.

**Kilbagie** *n.* In the 1780s Kilbagie in Clackmannanshire was the largest distillery in Scotland, developed by the whisky pioneer James Stein. Ironically, its vast production capacity was partly fuelled by the demand in London for bulk raw spirit that could be rectified for the growing gin market. By 1782 Kilbagie spirit exports to England amounted to 184,000 gallons. However, this Scottish gin production boom was short-lived due to an aggressive response and political lobbying campaign by London distillers. This produced a political backlash in England and led to the 1784 Wash Act which raised the duty on wash and a tax on export. This triggered a crash in the export trade which forced Stein to abandon the market and close down his Kilbagie gin production in 1787. Kilbagie then refocused on fast and efficient whisky production. This time Stein's innovation was the use of shallow pan-shaped stills to cook wash into spirit in minutes rather than hours. James Stein's successor Robert Stein brought this evolution to a new level in 1827 with the introduction of the world's first continuous still to be tested, passed and licensed by the Excise for distillation of whisky.

This drive for more efficient production and more capacity

contrasted with continued tradition in the Highlands of deep pot still malt production. In this way, a quality distinction emerged between Lowland and Highland distilleries. Kilbagie's continuous still production method was studied by the Irish Excise officer turned distiller Aeneas **Coffey** who refined the Kilbagie model further. In 1830, he produced the efficient Patent/Coffey continuous still design favoured by large grain distillers today.

**Kiln** *v.* To dry malted barley at the point when the germinating process has been triggered by steeping the barley or green malt. Timing is crucial to ensure that the maximum sugar yield is reached in each grain. Moisture level is a key factor in ensuring the dried malt is stored in a stable state and optimum condition for most efficient milling. Kilning halts the process at the perfect moisture level and starch levels for milling and removes and enhances flavouring compounds prior to distillation.

*n.* The distinctive pagoda roof profile is easily the most distinctive and recognisable architectural feature of any traditionally built malt whisky distillery. The louvred pagoda roof marks the malt kiln building which consists of three elements. The kiln furnace or oven on the ground floor is fired traditionally by coke, anthracite or peat. The wedge wire malt drying floor is above the furnace and the ventilating roof. The design of the steep pitched roof culminating in the louvred chimney head ensures that the smoke from the kiln, particularly the intense peat reek, vents outside by rising high and clear above the malt spread across the drying floor. Few distilleries kiln their own malt nowadays and pagoda roofs are now mere memorials and quaint features. Modern kilns are vast industrial buildings in purpose-built malting plants using natural gas heated malting floors.

**King's man** *n.* (Scots) Another of the many 19th century colloquial names used for the government's Excise Officers. Also known as the **Gauger** and the Exciseman.

## Kirsty

**Kirsty** *n.* (Scots) A traditional Scots colloquialism for a whisky jar.

**Knag** (also **Knaggie**) *n.* (Scots) A small wooden liquor vessel with a carry handle. A small keg or barrel.

**Knockin-mell** *n.* (Scots) A mallet for crushing and smashing husks of barley. Used in conjunction with the **Knockin-stane**.

**Knockin-stane** *n.* (Scots) The bowl-shaped stone mortar for collecting crushed barley husks, used in conjunction with the **Knockin-mell**.

# Low flyer

# L

**Label** *v. and n.* In bottling whisky, the act of placing a printed label on the bottle, also the act of creating a label design for a brand. The label must carry the mandatory descriptor which is required on every bottle of Scotch whisky. Scotch Whisky Regulation No 8 requires labels to state clearly the statutory notices of quantity, ABV % and producer of the contents. It must also state the category of Scotch Whisky using one of the appropriate definitions: *Single Malt, Scotch Whisky*, *Single Grain Scotch Whisky*, *Blended Scotch Whisky*, *Blended Malt Scotch Whisky* or *Blended Grain Scotch Whisky*. It is an offence to advertise or promote any Scotch whisky as belonging to a category to which it does not. The description must be given the same prominence as any other description of the whisky on the labels or packaging. The only word, or words, on the label which may be added to the category description are the name of the Scottish locality or region in which the Scotch whisky was distilled. For example, the description *Single Malt Scotch Whisky* must appear in exactly that form, except that it can also be preceded by a description such as *Speyside* or *Islay*, but only if that *Single Malt Scotch Whisky* has been entirely distilled in that region.

**Lace** *v.* To doctor or mix a spirit by adding tea or some other non-alcoholic beverage. Similarly, to doctor tea or non-alcoholic beverage by adding some tasteless spirit.

**Lag** *n.* In malting, the lag or air-rest is the second phase following the initial steeping of the barley grains to reach a moisture saturation of around 35%. In the lag phase the batch is drained and ventilated for ten hours to allow the moist grain membranes to soften. This encourages growth as the germination process and enzyme activity begin inside the grain. Germination occurs at this point as the roots and shoots chit and start to emerge from the germ of the grain. The third stage of the steeping soaks the batch again to maximise the water uptake and ensure the grain is fully hydrated and reaches the optimum 85% saturation.

**Laggin** *n.* (Scots) On a wooden barrel, cask or churn the laggin is the end of the stave where it projects beyond the bottom of the said wooden vessel. The lowermost metal hoop binding the barrel staves together.

**Laggin-gird** (also **Laggin-girtz**, **Legen-girtz**) *n.* (Scots) The bottom, or top, metal hoop which holds the wooden staves together in the construction of a traditional wooden barrel or cask.

**Lauter** *v.* To mash the malt, using the highly efficient mashing process adopted from the German brewing tradition. Lautering uses rotating steel combs to consistently stir the mash mix of grist and hot water round the mashing vessel. The rotating lauter arms ensure the liquid mix is continually agitated from top to bottom with the combs or blades separating the mix and avoiding clumping. This method of mashing is highly efficient in producing a sugar-rich wort liquid. This is drained for collection through the mashtun's finely perforated floors then filled into the washbacks for the next stage in the whisky making process. The remaining solids residue in the mashtun (draff) is pumped out and collected for transportation and processing into dry or wet agricultural feed.

**Lauter tun** *n.* Until the 1970s most distilleries used the traditional cast iron mash tun with rotating wooden paddles. The industry then began replacing these with the more efficient and consistent Lauter tun system developed for the brewing industry in Germany. The rotating lauter comb blades were found to be much more efficient than traditional paddles in their mashing effectiveness. Lauter blades can be raised, lowered and planed inside the closed steel mash tun to ensure maximum sugar extraction from the wort liquid. The design of the mild steel tuns also allows controlled sparge water flow, and much more precise temperature and flow management.

**Law** *n*. The earliest written records reveal that the Law has always shown a keen interest in whisky production in Scotland. In fact, it has shadowed the evolving art and craft of distilling aqua vitae/ uisge beatha from the Middle Ages monks of Lindores Abbey up to the industrial entrepreneurs of the Scottish Renaissance. A constant observer, the Law has been present to craft and shape its governance and ensure that a goodly share of the profits flows bountifully to the Treasury. Legal intervention began with the 1664 Excise Act which placed a new tax of two shillings and eight pence 'to be levied on every pint produced of aqua vitae'. Since then successive Acts of Parliament have ensured that every bottle of whisky produces a substantial government bounty which in 2017 stands at 76% of the bottle price.

Perhaps surprisingly the first legal definition of Scotch whisky was only laid down in 1909 following the findings of the *Royal Commission on Whiskey and other potable Spirits*. This definition has continued to be amended and strengthened over the years domestically and internationally with recognition in EU legislation from 1989 and the 2009 Scotch Whisky Regulations. In 2012, the Regulations were tightened by requiring all Single Malt Scotch Whisky to be bottled in Scotland. This review also defined how Scotch whisky is presented and the appropriate wording for descriptions on labelling, packaging and advertising. Under the Regulations Scotch Whisky is defined as whisky:

- Which has been produced at a distillery in Scotland from water and malted barley (to which only whole grains of other cereals may be added) all of which have been:
- Processed at that distillery into a mash,
- Converted to a fermentable substrate only by endogenous enzyme systems, Fermented only by the addition of yeast,
- Distilled at an alcoholic strength by volume of less than 94.8% so the distillate has an aroma and taste derived from the raw materials used in, and the method of, its production,
- Matured in an excise warehouse in Scotland in oak casks of a capacity not exceeding seven hundred litres, the period of that maturation being not less than three years.
- Retains only the colour, aroma, and taste derived from the raw materials used in, and the method of, its production and maturation.
- Contains no substance other than water and plain caramel.

**Legs** *n.* Clinging oily streaks of the spirit which visibly coat the sides when undiluted whisky is poured and swilled around a glass. Legs are a clear visual indication of the weight or heaviness of the spirit. The addition of even just a splash of water disrupts the surface tension and the whisky loses its distinctive legs.

**Leucine** *n.* One the slower group of amino acids absorbed early in the fermentation process. Together with **histidine**, **isoleucine**, **methionine** and **valine** these are first to be synthesised as the yeast works in the washback, feeding and expanding on the sugar in the wort.

**Lignin** *n.* Comprising 22-25% of oak wood material, lignin contributes much of the significant flavour compounds derived from maturing spirit in oak casks. These compounds are only made accessible to the spirit if the casks have been toasted or charred by direct flame. At the charred or toasted layer of the wood these flavour compounds are released and interact with the spirit to influence flavour in the early stages of maturation and quickly reach their flavour threshold in the whisky. Lignin's background presence deeper into the oak wood continues to make it a long-term influencer on the whisky's finished flavour as the spirit seeps deeper during maturation. Indeed, its robust presence can still be traced working in older, used whisky casks, showing how deeply the lignin influence lies in the maturation of whisky.

**Lindores Abbey** *n.* Founded in 1191, Lindores Abbey on the outskirts of Newburgh in Fife is one of the most important historic sites for Scotch whisky scholars. It is famously identified as the oldest recorded distiller of aqua vitae and therefore, in written history at least, the recognised progenitor of all Scotch Whisky. Records in the Exchequer Rolls dated June 1st, 1494 show that James IV commissioned the Tironensian abbey's **Friar John Cor** to make whisky. The Tironensians were skilled alchemists and apothecaries and King James IV granted the abbey rights to make aqua vitae to supply his hunting lodge at nearby Falkland Palace. His order reads: *'To brother John Cor, by order of the King, to make aqua vitae, VIII bolls of malt'.*

Unfortunately, the abbey was sacked by John Knox and his supporters in 1559 and thereafter plundered for its finished stone, wooden panels and other features. Thankfully many of these have survived and can be seen incorporated into other historic buildings around Fife and Dundee. The poignant and still beautiful ruins of Lindores are now a shrine of pilgrimage for Scotch whisky lovers from all over the world who travel to the site for a moment of contemplation, a salute to Friar John Cor and enjoyment of a dram in gratitude for Scotland's gift to the world. At time of writing a new distillery is being constructed here, invoking the spirit of John Cor once again on the site and reviving the ancient tradition of distilling at Lindores.

# Line

**Line** *n.* The abbreviated name for the boundary that defines the beginning and end of the **Highland** defined whisky region.

**Liquefy** *v.* (Scots) To spend money on, or change money for, alcoholic drink or liquor.

**Liqueurs** *n.* Specialist recipe blended drinks mixing whisky with 'complementary' flavourings. Perhaps best known is **Drambuie** with its secret recipe supposedly handed down from Bonnie Prince Charlie. There are many others which stretch and challenge the boundaries of the whisky lover's taste buds. These include cinnamon flavoured *Fireball* and *Fire Eater*, bacon flavoured *Ol' Major Bacon Bourbon, New York Apple Flavoured Whisky, Sasanokawa Cherry Ex Whisky Liqueur* and *Mackmyra Bee Honey Whisky Liqueur*.

**Locality** *n.* Scotch whisky production is defined and divided in terms of the geographic locality where it is distilled. The localities are the regions of *Highlands and Islands, Lowland, Speyside, Islay and Campbeltown,* which can be used to precede the category description on labels. Thus, a Single Malt Scotch Whisky distilled in the Highland region may be described on the label as *Highland Single Malt Scotch Whisky*, etc. Regulations state that the words must appear in exactly that order or appear separately from the category description, provided as they are no more prominent than that description.

**Loch Lomond** – see **Grain distilleries**

**Lost Distillery** *adj.* A closed, converted or demolished distillery which cannot be revived to production. With well over a hundred lost distilleries across Scotland, the finite stocks of whisky they produced means their bottlings have a special collectability - and price. As an example, when in 2014 Diageo released 'Brora 40' from the distillery which closed in 1983 they confidently attached a price tag of £6,995 per bottle.

**Low Flyer** *n.* A popular Scottish colloquialism used when one is ordering a measure of the iconic brand, *The Famous Grouse*. In production since 1896, The Famous Grouse is one of the oldest blend brands and famously includes Macallan and Highland Park single malts among the 40 or so whiskies in the blend recipe. Traditionally heard in working class pubs, a *Low Flyer* is often paired with a glass of dark beer as in: *A wee heavy and a low flyer*, meaning a half of Scotch ale (7-10%) with a quarter gill chaser of Famous Grouse.

**Lowland** *n. and adj.* Lowland is one of Scotland's protected regions which define geographic areas with their own distinctive style and character. It comprises the part of Scotland that is south of a line roughly from Dundee in the East to Greenock in the West, dividing it from the Highland region. Lowland whiskies present a spirit with a light, delicate flavour. They were previously distinguished by being traditionally triple distilled to produce flavour notes on tasting are floral, light and sweet. Today the only Scottish distillery continuing with a triple distillation process is Auchentoshan.

**Lowland still** *n.* Also known as the Shallow still. A type of still which was designed to circumvent government legislation which calculated spirit duty on still size and an estimated filling and running of seven times a week. The Lowland still's design was a pan shaped still that was wide and shallow which meant it could be run extremely fast and often. The wash filled the pan just a few inches deep and usually just about over the minimum legal capacity with heated coils forcing the evaporation. It was claimed the Lowland still could run a batch of spirit in three minutes which meant huge efficiency gains over the pot still but produced a fiery spirit much coarser than the Highland or pot still.

**Low Wines** *n.* The fortified alcoholic liquor produced following the first distillation of the wash in the wash still. The quantity of liquor this produces for the second distillation measures around 40% of the volume of the original wash charge. Low Wines are run from the wash still condenser through the spirit safe to a stainless steel reservoir, called the *low wines and feints receiver*. This Low Wines liquor has an ABV of around 21-25% and is held in the receiver until it is filled to the ABV level required to run through the second distillation in the spirit still.

**Lum** *n.* (Scots) The characteristic tall, free standing brick chimney stack at the heart of any of the sprawling, coalfired distilleries built in the 19th century. These towering industrial lums became incongruous features of some surprisingly remote areas throughout rural Scotland as they vented black smoke from their coal furnaces. Their appearance coincided with the coming of the railway. The railway enabled cost-effective bulk transport of coal, coke and anthracite, meaning distilleries could be founded in remoter locations along the railway lines where land and labour was cheap, and water and peat fuel plentiful.

**Lush** *n.* Anyone who is known to habitually and regularly drink alcohol. Also any alcoholic drink or strong liquor.

**Lyne-arm** (also **Lyin-arm**, **Lain-arm** or **Lye Pipe**) *n.* (Scots) This piece of still apparatus is another key influencer on the character and flavour of any distillery's spirit. Usually tapered, cylindrical and angled, the lyne-arm is the copper continuation of the top of the pot still. Each distillery has its own signature angle, shape, bore and length of lyne-arm designed to add subtle and distinctive flavour notes to the spirit. The lyne-arm channels rising hot alcohol vapour from the top of the still across and down into the cooling worm or **condenser**. Here it reforms, or condenses as low wines or liquid spirit. The copper surface of the lyne-arm also acts as a secondary reflux, interacting with the vapours as they travel to the condenser. Here further complex interactions take place forming esters, flavour **congeners** that establish fruity, winey notes in the spirit. Most ester creation happens in the larger copper chamber of the still but the lyne-arm adds additional subtle esters just at the point before ethanol vapour condenses to liquid form.

# M

**Magnum Bonum** *n.* A traditional Scottish bottle for wine or whisky containing two quarts or around 2.2 litres of liquor.

**Maiser** (also **Mazer**) *n.* (Scots) A traditional drinking cup made of maple wood.

**Malt** *n.* One of the essential primary ingredients in the malt whisky recipe. Malt is the dry storable grain product derived after the barley has been steeped and germinated to produce rootlets and shoots or **cuilms**. The maltase enzyme in the kernel triggers production of the key sugar compound maltose in the barley grain. At this growth stage the barley is referred to as green malt, i.e. barley which has been processed to the optimum germination condition, but has not yet been kilned and is still actively growing. The barley is now kiln dried to halt the growth process in readiness for storage and transport.

**Maltase** *n.* The enzyme produced in the barley grain when hydrolysis and heat trigger germination and malting. Maltase releases the sugars in the grain's nucleus and husk. Its action causes the splitting of the maltose sugar compound in the barley, releasing two versions of the glucose molecule.

**Malt Barn** *n.* Easily recognised in older distilleries by their traditional roofline topped by a vented 'pagoda', the malt barn was built to accommodate the steeping, resting, germinating and kilning processes under one roof. They remain a common sight but few malt distilleries use these iconic buildings for their original purpose today. Instead they are retained as treasured architectural features reflecting the evolution of the working distillery. Most distilleries today use bulk malt produced and supplied by one of Scotland's specialist industrial malt suppliers such as Bairds or Simpsons whose HGV wagons are a constant feature on the main trunk roads from the Borders to the Northern and Western Isles.

**Malt Bins** *n.* The huge steel hoppers used for storage of malt. The malt bins in each distillery are designed and located to maintain the necessary cool, dry conditions to keep the malted barley in condition. With an average capacity of 50 tonnes, the inverted pyramid shape enables gravity to power the flow of dry malt. Measured batches of malt are delivered via a conveyor belt system from the bin into the mill hopper then to the **Malt Mill** before supplying milled malt to the grist hopper in the mash room.

**Malt Distillers Association of Scotland** *n.* A trade organisation that exists to represent the views and interests of nearly all companies which operate malt whisky distilleries across Scotland. By 2016 there were 83 operational malt whisky distilleries with the greatest concentrations in and around Speyside (45) and Islay (8). The total number of distilleries is now rising significantly with the arrival of a buoyant small to medium sized craft distillery sector. A number of new distilleries are scheduled to open with many new projects breaking soil in 2017.

**Malting Drums** *n.* Also known as Germination and Kilning Vessels (**GKVs**) or Steeping, Germination and Kilning Vessels (SGKVs). Vast, temperature controlled, rotating sealed steel chambers designed to trigger and control germination of large batches of barley. In comparison with the traditional **Saladin box** or vat germination, the GKV malting drums' slow, gentle *rotation*, *agitation* and temperature controlled *aeration* efficiently produces malt of a very high and consistent standard. The even transfer and efficient control of temperature and humidity over four days creates optimum conditions for barley germination with minimal damage to the rootlets, producing green malt and perfect conditions for kilning.

**Maltman** *n.* Malting is a key craft in the creation of fine Scotch whisky. The role oversees all the important changes occurring in the barley grains, through the steeping, resting, germination and kilning processes. The malt man or woman ensures the barley reaches optimum malting condition over a six-day period. Only when he or she is satisfied that the barley is ready will it be released for storage in the distillery's malt bins.

**Maltman's Rub** *n.* A traditional test for condition of malt grains. The maltman will take a sample from deep within the batch and firmly rub the grains between the thumb and forefinger. This is the final key test of readiness and quality of a batch of malt which has been steeped, germinated and finally kilned. If the batch is in prime condition the grain husks will break apart easily and coat his fingers with the fine, white powdery starch inside.

**Malt Mill** *n.* Carefully calibrated steel rollers crack open the barley grains to release the white powdery starch from the husk. Before milling, the malt grains are passed through the malt mill screen filters to remove any stones or foreign matter and dried cuilms. The kernels are then crushed into grist between two sets of finely adjusted horizontal steel rollers before being conveyed to the grist hopper. The setting of the malt mill rollers is key. Grist that is too coarse produces less fermentable material resulting in reduced alcohol yield. Too fine and the grist causes sludging in the mash, making it difficult to drain through the lauter tun and a loss of overall alcohol yield.

**Maltose** *n.* The sugar compound accessed by the starch breakdown in the barley during malting. The compound consists of two molecules of glucose which are split by the enzyme maltase as the grain germinates.

**Marriage** *n*. Marriage is the process whereby matured single malt whiskies from two or more casks are brought together in larger oak tuns or vats. The marrying technique was developed as a way of smoothing out flavour differences between whiskies from the same batch, but matured in different casks. Marrying combines the flavour characteristics of the whiskies until they stabilise. The marriage can last weeks, months or even years until the malt master is satisfied that the combination has achieved its optimum settled flavour and the whisky is ready for bottling. The term is also used in blended whiskies when the selected malt and grain whiskies have been brought together for the first time in a butt or vat. The blend marriage is then allowed to rest for a period of weeks to settle and take on its settled character before bottling.

**Mash** *v*. To cook the grist of the malted barley. Mashing takes place inside a mashtun vessel in the mash house or mash room. A mashing will take around six hours based on an average batch of eight tonnes of grist malt. This is mixed one part grist to four parts water. A batch of grist of this size will be cooked using around 45,500 litres of water, starting at the optimum *sugar-extracting* temperature of 64.5oC. Inside the mashtun the rotating lauter blades mix the grist to ensure maximum sugar dissolution. The mashing process is marked by four water stages; first water at 64.5 oC, second water at 70 oC, third water at 80 oC and fourth water at 90 oC. These increasing cooking temperatures ensure that every last molecule of the grist is utilised. The first two waters *cook* the grist producing a sugary solution for the next fermentation stage. The lower sugar content of the third and fourth sparging waters 'mop up' any remaining sugar and are recycled for use as part of the first water in the next mashing batch. The process produces **wort** liquor, rich in maltose and glucose fermentable sugars. Before the next stage the wort liquor stands for over an hour. Then it is drawn off, cooled and sent to the washback fermentation vessels. The solids residue left in the mashtun is **draff**, a sweet 'porridge' that is drained and pumped out for transportation and processing as cattle feed.

**Mash House** (also **Mash Room**) *n*. The room or chamber within the distillery housing all the vessels, controls and plant for the mashing. This includes the mashtun, underback, grist hopper and all pipework for sending the wort and draff products to the next stage.

**Mashlach** (also **Mashlam**, **Mashlie**) *n*. (Scots) Any batch of mixed grains, a mixture of barley, wheat, corn etc.

**Mashman** *n*. Traditional name for the person whose job it is to run the mashing process from start to finish, transforming malted barley into sugar rich wort liquor and the draff cattle feed by- product.

**Mashtun** *n*. Mashtuns were once large, open, cast-iron vessels in which the mash was stirred manually using long-handled paddles. Mechanisation removed the manual labour, then from the 1970s the traditional open cast-iron mash tun came to be replaced by more efficient sealed steel **Lauter** tuns. These mild steel mashing vessels delivered continuous sparge water flow and temperature control and used rotating lauter blades or knives that can be raised, lowered and planed to ensure the maximum agitation of the liquid mix. Perforated plates in the floor of the mashtun have slits which filter the mix, enabling the wort liquid to drain off and be pumping through to the wash room for fermentation.

**Mask** *v*. (Scots) To mash, to cook malted barley for brewing, also to brew tea.
   *n*. The action of brewing.

**Mask knife** *n*. The vertical blade on the rotating arm inside a lauter mashtun. Fixed in an array, they sift through the mash as the arms turn. The angle of the mask knives can be planed or adjusted to suit the requirements of the mash man.

**Maturation** *n.* The process by which new-make spirit from the pot or patent stills is transformed into legally saleable Scotch whisky. Maturation must take place in oak casks after the new- make spirit has been diluted to 64.5% ABV before filling into the cask. Over the years, the spirit's interaction with the oak wood adds desirable flavours, removes undesirable flavours, and creates unique new flavours. Many factors will influence the maturation of the clear spirit as it takes on colour, flavour and character from the wood and the climatic conditions around it. It is thought that as much as 70% of the flavour is drawn from the oak wood, the cask type and its previous use. For certification as Scotch whisky, maturation must take place in a warehouse in Scotland regulated by HMRC.

**Maut** (also **Mauten**) *v.* (Scots) To soak, germinate and dry barley grains once they have produced roots and shoots or cuilms. To germinate grains, to produce malt by sprouting roots and shoots.
*n.* Whisky. Malted barley grain, ready for milling to grist before it is mashed, fermented and distilled into spirit.

**Maut-bree** *n.* (Scots) Malt liquor. Spirit.

**Maut-kiln** *n.* (Scots) The kiln for drying malt, fired by peat, coal or anthracite.

**Mautman** *n.* (Scots) The maltster who oversees and controls the malting process of the barley from start to finish.

**Meal-and-ale** *n.* (Scots) A traditional mixture of oatmeal, ale, sugar and whisky made up to celebrate the final cutting and gathering in of the grain harvest.

**Medicine** *n*. In Scotland, stocks of whisky miniatures are routinely kept in hospitals for prescription and administration to inpatients for medicinal purposes. During the United States years of **Prohibition** between 1920 and 1933, Scots whisky producers successfully maintained their export sales to the US by having whisky designated as a medicine. Doctors were free to habitually prescribe *medicinal liquor* to their patients as a treatment for conditions such as indigestion, cancer and depression. Doctors received $3 per prescription and the patients would pay around $3-4 to be supplied with a pint of their liquor of choice. Of course, the restorative powers of whisky had long been recognised in Scotland. In the 19th century Pattisons Distillers produced a blended whisky called *The Doctor* which was supplied sealed inside a ceramic jar marked with a red cross on the side.

**Meridian** *n*. (Scots) The City of Edinburgh tradition for those working on trades and crafts in the town, of partaking of a mid-day dram. Dating back to the 18th century, the sounding of the bells of St Giles Cathedral ahead of 12 noon was the signal to the working folk of the city. Tradesmen and workers would down their tools and head for their local inn or tavern for one or two drams of whisky and a tassie of porter to ready them for the trials of the rest of the day.

**Methionine** *n*. Methionine belongs to the group of amino acids slowly absorbed in the early stage of the fermentation process. It is synthesised as the yeast in the washback feeds and expands on the sugar in the wort. The group also includes histidine, isoleucine, leucine and valine.

**Mettin** *n*. (Scots) An ear or grain of barley.

**Millroom** *n*. In older distilleries the millroom was at the centre of the buildings on the ground floor. Here rotating friction rollers would grind the malt into grist for conveying on elevator belts up to the grist room. Here the grist would be kept cool and dry until required for the next mashing.

# Ming

**Ming** *v. and n.* (Scots) To give off an odour. To smell. A mix or blend. A smell.

**Miroculous** *adj.* (Scots) Very drunk. Incoherent due to alcohol intoxication.

**Mixed** *adj.* (Scots) Muddled with drink.

**Moffat Meisur** *n.* (Scots) A generous pouring or measure.

**Molass** (also **Molash**) *n.* (Scots) Spirits distilled from molasses. Much of the production of Indian whisky nowadays is derived from distilled molasses.

**Monkey Shoulder** *n.* A repetitive strain condition unique to maltmen working in traditional malting floors in distilleries. This classic musculo-skeletal ailment is caused by years of wielding the malt shiel (Scots) or shovel, from left to right, sifting and turning the mounds of barley grains in the malt barns to ensure moisture consistency.

**Moonshine** *n.* The high-proof spirits distilled in certain parts of the United States. Also known as *Hooch, Mountain Dew, White Whiskey, White Lightning, Homebrew, Corn liquor* etc. Typically made using a corn mash as the main ingredient, moonshine is especially associated with the Appalachian Mountains where the art of making white whiskey arrived with the Scots, Ulster-Scots and Irish immigrants who arrived in the late 18th and early 19th centuries. They brought over with them their skills and recipes for making raw, un-aged whisky and this became the trademark method of producing spirit in the Appalachian area. The romantic name 'moonshine' reflects the fact that the distillers and distributors traditionally kept their operations nocturnal and secretive to avoid discovery. Today these spirits are still often illicitly distilled but there are also legal,

commercial brands on sale. Illicit distilling in the United States is
pursued by the Department of Justice Bureau of Alcohol, Tobacco,
Firearms and Explosives whose officers are traditionally known as
the *revenooers*.

**Morning** (also **Morning-drink**) *n.* (Scots) The fortifying tradition
of taking a glass of whisky or brandy before breakfast.

**Mortal-fou** *adj.* (Scots) 'Dead' drunk. Immobilised by alcohol
intoxication

**Mother** *n.* (Scots) In the brewing or fermentation of wort inside the
washbacks, the *'mother of the beer'* is the lees of the yeast. This is the
thick foamy froth that forms and rises to the top of the wash ale in
the vessel.

**Moulie-drops** *n.* (Scots) Drops of liquor left over in the bottom of
a glass. Dregs.

**Muddy** *adj.* (Scots) Not lucid, befuddled. Muddled with drink.

**Muskin** *n.* (Scots) A traditional liquid or drink measure consisting of
four Scots gills amounting to a quarter pint Scots or an English pint.

**Musty** *adj.* Undesirable stale taste or odour identifiable from mould
or decay that sometimes carries through from the porous oak wood
to the maturing spirit. If, alas, it is apparent when the bottle is
opened and the whisky is poured then it renders all the years and
best efforts of the distiller wasted in the cask.

**Mutchkin-bottle** (also **Mutchkin-cup, Mutchkin-stoup**) *n.*
(Scots) A vessel sized to measure or hold a mutchkin or quarter
pint Scots.

# Noggin

# N

**Naked truth** *n*. (Scots) Whisky or indeed any other spirit poured and drunk neat and undiluted.

**Nale** *n*. (Scots) An ale house.

**Naming** *n*. Much time and care goes into making whisky, so it is only right that the distiller, blender or retailer applies similar craft and sensitivity in choosing a name before sending it out into the world. Traditionally it was simple. Whiskies were simply named after the distillery, the distiller or the distillery owner. In the mid-19th century matters changed with the arrival of the blend. Now there was a growing market for whisky created by vatting together individual whiskies from twenty and more sources. These new blends couldn't reflect an individual source but instead required names reflecting the recipe or market it was aimed at. Global expansion created a new fashion for inventing brand names to match the blended whisky's character and so the famous global brands were born: *Johnnie Walker, VAT '69, J&B Rare, The Antiquary, Dimple, Chivas Regal, Cutty Sark, The Famous Grouse* and more.

In the 20th century the blended market share was dominant and international growth following the end of American Prohibition in 1933 meant blenders' recipes and even bottle shapes, had to be securely protected. In the single malt market the traditional naming protocol of distillery name and cask age of the whisky continued throughout the 20th century. In the early 21st century, we are in the midst of a worldwide growth in demand for single malts across the globe. This demand has driven a new trend for bringing younger expressions of the classic malt distilleries onto the market before the traditional 12 year plus releases. Now, rather than the traditional age statement we see famous distillery names releasing comparatively young single malts with romantic, colourful and even amusing names such as: *Talisker Storm, Macallan Gold, Jura Superstition, Tomatin Cù Bocan,* etc.

**Nap** (also **Napper**) *n.* (Scots) The head. In drink, the head of a poured ale. A strong beer. The brain. Common Scots usage might be for example; '*I had to use my napper to get roon it*' referring to the need to deploy advanced strategic thinking to circumvent an obstacle and make due progress.

**Naphtha** *n.* A highly flammable liquid which can be distilled from naturally occurring hydrocarbons such as peat. In 1877 duty was abolished for distilled spirits that had been methylated by the addition of the highly flammable wood naphtha solvent. This removal of duty encouraged distillers to prioritise the production of potent, patent grain whisky over malt whisky.

**Napoleon** *n.* Despite his association with the eponymous brandy, Emperor Napoleon also cast his influence on the production of whisky in Scotland for the duration of the Napoleonic Wars, especially the years 1809-11. A British ban on trade with France coincided with a series of disastrous years for the Scottish grain harvest. Napoleon had also placed a stranglehold on European trade with Britain through the 1807 Treaty of Tilsit agreed with Tsar Alexander I of Russia. This effectively blockaded Britain from trading with the continent. This so disrupted the supply of grain that all use for distilling spirit was banned in favour of food production until the defeat of France in 1815. One upside to the Napoleonic Wars was the opportunity presented for popularising whisky. Due to the unavailability of French brandy and continental Cognac imports there was a great upsurge domestically in demand for good whisky. This triggered an historic change in drawing-room tastes in the British Isles for Scotch over brandy which survives to this day.

**Nappie** *n.* (Scots) Any rich, strong ale. *adj.* Of drink or liquor, intoxicating. Heady. Heavy. Foaming. Also of people, tipsy. Squiffy. Overly exuberant with drink.

**Nauber** *adj.* (Scots) Being overly parsimonious or mean. Stingy, given to giving short measure.

**Navigation Acts** *n.* Acts put in place in 1651 as protectionist measures to keep at bay the *'enemies'* of the British Empire and limit trade with the British colonies. By 1849 these were deemed to be counter-productive and the repeal of the Navigation Acts removed historic limiting measures and restrictions. This opened up new markets, encouraged expanded production of grain whisky at home and enabled export to new territories abroad.

**Neck** *v.* (Scots) To crack the neck of a bottle to access the contents. To drain the contents of a bottle or drinking vessel at a single swallowing.
　　*n.* A feature of still design. The length and width of the neck on the head of a still influences the eventual character and flavour of the whisky. Stills with short wide necks tend to yield heavier, more oily whisky. Stills with tall narrow necks yield whisky which is light in character and delicately flavoured.

**Newhaven-gill** *n.* (Scots) A traditional Scottish measure of liquor of two gills or 284 millilitres. It takes its name from the fishing village of Newhaven on the shores of the Forth to the north of Edinburgh. Founded by the Scottish King James IV in 1504 as a base for building a royal Scottish navy, Newhaven was soon populated by fishing families. The menfolk became known for their navigation skills on the Firth of Forth and further out into the North Sea. The size of the measure poured in the Newhaven-gill reflected both the relief at a successful return from the sea and the need to steady the resolve ahead of embarking on the next voyage out into the Forth.

**Newing** *n*. (Scots) The frothy head or *barm* that forms on top of the wash ale in the washback, caused by the fermenting action of the yeast working on the sugars in the wort to create alcohol.

**New-make spirit** *n*. Also known as *new distillate*. The finished product sent to the spirit receiver at the end of the spirit run. New-make is diluted with water down to 64.5% ABV before being put into the cask for maturation. Normally a batch of new-make spirit will be assessed before committing to a cask by the **nosers** of the company. This is done by pouring 25ml samples of new-make spirit diluted with distilled water down to 20% ABV. The sample is covered by a watch glass for half an hour to capture and intensify the odours and allow aromas to coalesce. An individual noser or panel of nosers will then assess the new-make by eye and by nose before recording their critiques and recommendations for cask maturation. These would include preferences of cask type best suited to maturing and producing the distiller's desired outcome in whisky style.

**Nick** *v*. (Scots) To drink a glass to the finish enthusiastically and heartily.

**Nineteenth Hole** *n*. Colloquialism for the bar of a golf clubhouse and the final destination of any round of golf. With a round consisting of 18 holes the game is only completed at the ceremonial sinking in the 19th hole of the winner's dram. A popular tradition with all in the clubhouse as this is traditionally sunk at the expense of the winner.

**Nip** *n*. (Scots) A single, satisfying measure of whisky. In Scotland, a nip is traditionally a quarter gill or 35 millilitres and poured in a small nip glass or shot glass.

**Nitrogen** *n*. The presence of nitrogen in the barley level of its content is a key influence on the eventual spirit yield of a batch of malt. The higher the nitrogen content of the wort at the brewing stage, the greater the amount of yeast cell growth. This has an impact on the amount of spirit yielded and distilled from a batch. The higher the proportion of the fermentable sugars used up in cell growth, the less is available for producing *ethanol*.

**No.10** *n*. In the late 19th and early 20th century production of grain whisky boomed on the back of the growing export market for blended Scotch whisky. The popularity of blends meant the arrival of the twin necessary evils of marketing and branding to connect brands with new customers and gain their brand loyalty. One of the more audacious brand names was *'No.10'* by James Watson of Dundee. The naming and marketing deliberately promoting the brand as belonging in the Downing Street drinks cabinet of the Prime Minister of Great Britain.

**Noddelt** *adj*. (Scots) Meaning just as it sounds when spoken. Completely muddled by drink. Confused. Befuddled.

**Noggin** *n*. A small cup or generous loose measure of spirit, traditionally around a gill (142 ml). Colloquially, also the head. Or at least the bit that houses the strategic and rational functions of the brain. Often used by those claiming to display a particularly successful application of intelligence to a problem.

**Noitled** *adj*. (Scots) Drunk. Under the influence of spirits. Befuddled.

**Norland Blue** *n*. (Scots) Lowlander's name for Highland whisky.

## North British Distillery

*Norland* is another Scots language name for the 'North-land' or the Gaelic-speaking Highlands and *blue* a colloquial name for new-make spirit.

**North British Distillery** *n*. One of the seven large grain distilleries in Scotland, commonly called the 'NB'. Famously directly linked to the first successful blended whisky brand Usher's. Founded in 1885 by Edinburgh whisky blenders and wine and spirit merchants **Andrew Usher**, William Sanderson and John Crabbie. The NB distillery was primarily built as a guaranteed source of supply for their own businesses in the face of the growing market dominance of the recently formed conglomerate Distillers Company. The new production facility in the Gorgie and Dalry district the city was a counter to their strength and the NB opened in 1887. Today the NB is Scotland's second oldest and second biggest grain distillery, producing 64 million litres of alcohol per annum. In 2015 it celebrated producing its historic 2.5 billionth cask.

**Nose** *n*. The aroma from the vapour of a whisky once poured. The olfactory organ plays a major role in the appreciation of whisky. It makes the first sensory encounter and kicks off the process of identifying the origin, character and qualities of the spirit. Any whisky producer needs and values having a sensitive, skilled and experienced noser on the payroll and especially in the blending room. Once a whisky has been poured, preferably into a tulip-shaped glass, and the vapour released, the nose acts as a diviner, analysing and discerning each element of the spectrum of aromas.

**Noser** *n*. The person in any whisky producing operation who is regarded as having the most sensitive and discerning olfactory skills. These are valued for analysing the component aromas and flavours and rating the quality of a whisky. Also (Scots) A head-on blizzard. Extremely wild and dangerous weather conditions.

**Note** *n.* In tastings, the individual, elemental components of a whisky's flavour. Identified and described as *notes* or *flavour notes*. A popular feature of a whisky tasting for participants is identifying and recording flavour note opinions and reactions on *tasting note sheets* for each whisky sampled.

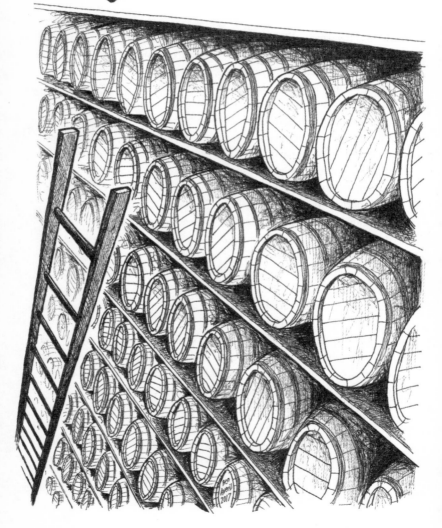
REACHING FOR THE HIGH OCTAVE

# O

**Oak** *n.* The source of much of the character of any cask matured Scotch whisky and one of the signature whisky flavours in the distiller's palette. The magical flavouring qualities derived from filling liquor into breathing oak wood casks was recognised two thousand years ago by the expanding Roman empire. As they invaded northern Europe the inquisitive Romans were intrigued by the *Gauls'* practice of using oak casks to store and transport their liquor. Compared with the properties of the legions' traditional hermetically-sealed ceramic *amphorae* the wood cask proved both more practical and enhancing to the flavour of the liquor. The maturation effect and flavouring properties of oak on liquor has long since been studied and is now understood at its most detailed organic chemistry levels. It is reckoned that as much as 70% of the flavour and character of the whisky is derived from its interaction with the wood as the spirit matures in the cask. Over the centuries, the planting and harvesting of oak wood has been carefully nurtured to ensure quality oak casks continue to be supplied to wine and spirit producers.

For the past 500 years only oak wood from trees between 70 and 200 years has been used for cask production. Three types of oak wood are used: American white oak **Quercus Alba**, European white oak **Quercus Robur**, and Mizunara or Japanese oak, **Quercus Mongolica**. Each is said to have different characteristics. American white oak grows faster and produces a mellower, finer and more focused aroma than the Japanese or European oak. While an American oak can be taken for cask making after seventy

# Oak lactones

years, the slower growing European oak must be left for around one hundred and fifty years. The Japanese oak wood interacts with the spirit at a different rate and so more maturing time is required in the cask. An important step in readying a newly finished oak cask is the flaming and charring of the inside to open the surface and release the distinctive sweet, caramel, vanilla and toasted aromas. Charred oak contributes a deeper colour than uncharred oak. However, uncharred oak delivers very distinct coconut and cloves flavours as well as a characteristically lighter lemony colour tone. Other hard woods have been tried but the flavouring results were found to be less than pleasant. As for softwoods, being resinous they are useless as they don't allow the cask to breathe. They also contribute an unwelcome astringency.

**Oak lactones** *n.* Oak lactones are the key flavour elements harbouring within the cask wood. They are credited with contributing as much as 70% of the flavour of the finished whisky. The casks are charred by direct flame or oven baked to break the surface integrity of the wood membrane and allow the spirit to access the lactones and interact with these compounds. As the spirit soaks in, over time the lactones will give off the characteristic aroma associated with oak casks. These are typically flavour notes of coconut, toastiness, vanilla and wood sugars, as well as a distinctive lemony or straw colour.

**Obscuration** *n.* There are two ways of sampling the same batch of liquor for the purpose of estimating the *apparent* and *real* alcohol content (ABV). These samplings are done before and after distillation of the liquor. For the apparent alcohol content a *non-distilled* sample of liquor from the batch is tested. The real alcoholic strength is determined by testing the liquor after distillation. Before distillation, the liquor carries dissolved solids which increase the density of the liquor and obscure the accurate measurement of likely ABV to the point of reducing it. This obscuration means the pre-distilled sample measurement shows only its apparent alcoholic strength. The clear post-distilled sample measurement will show the real alcoholic strength of a batch of spirit. The purpose of these measurements is to determine the amount of alcohol likely to be produced from a batch and so calculate likely excise duty to be paid to HMRC.

**Octave** *n.* One of the smallest traditional whisky cask sizes still in commercial use with a capacity of fifty litres of spirit.

**Octomore** *n.* (Scots, from the Scots Gaelic ***Ochdamh-Mor*** 'The Big Eighth'). Distilled on Islay at Bruichladdich distillery, the Octomore is claimed to be the world's most heavily-peated whisky with a distilled spirit peat trace varying up to 167 parts per million (ppm) compared to other traditionally heavily peated Islay malts sitting at around 40 ppm. In a long-matured whisky lying in a cask for 12 years this would produce an overwhelming intensity of wood and smoke in the whisky. However, Octomore is deliberately bottled young at around five years. This dilutes the weighty peatiness by shortening and lightening the spirit's cask finish. The whisky itself is named in tribute to the nearby Octomore farm which housed its own distillery in 1816, long before the arrival of the builders at Bruichladdich.

**O'ertake** *v.* (Scots) To become suddenly drunk, e.g. *Sandy aye gie's us a sang when the uisge beatha o'ertakes him.* Sandy always gives us a song when he gets drunk on whisky.

**O'ertap** *v.* (Scots) To overfill a glass or vessel causing spillage of good liquor, e.g. *Ye've o'ertapped it ya muckle clunker!* You've overfilled it you clumsy oaf!

**Off-odours** *n.* Any traces of unwelcome or spoiling aromas apparent when a bottle of whisky is opened or poured. Usually an off-odour is a rank mustiness or mothball ming. This occurs if the whisky is stored for too long in an atmosphere of wet and hot or humid storage conditions. These conditions can degrade any cardboard or fibrous components of the packaging, releasing trichloranisole microbes into the atmosphere around the bottle. These microbes can pass through the bottle seal, fouling the whisky inside. Another off-odour has its source before packaging, at the very start of the distilling process. Any barley or cereals kept in damp storage conditions before fermentation can suffer from bacterial growth. Unhindered this can progress to spoil the entire batch by creating the earthy smelling compound **geosmin**. If undetected, geosmin can pass through the entire distillation and maturation process until the day the whisky cask is opened and the fouled whisky odour hits the nose. Geosmin is familiar to most of us as the cause of *petrichor*, that musky, earthy smell that hangs in the air after heavy rainfall.

**Ogie** (also **Oggie**) *n.* (Scots) The open floor space used for shovelling, stoking and fire management by the stokers at the mouth or fireplace of the oven of a malt kiln.

**Oil** *n.* Oil is one of the by-products of the continuous grain whisky patent distillation process. *Feint oil* is a run-off from the continuous distillation process. With a minimal ethanol/alcohol content of around 1%, the feint oil can to be sold as a nutrient rich by-product fusel oil.

**Oiliness** *n.* The viscosity of a whisky as observed in the glass. One of the key visual characteristics together with depth of colour for assessing the quality of a poured whisky. A whisky's weight and density can be clearly seen in the oily streaks, or legs, it leaves as gravity drags the spirit down the glass. The addition of a bead of water from a beaked jug or pipette will break this viscosity to open a second layer of flavour beneath the oiliness.

**Oil of malt** *n.* (Scots) A whisky distilled from malt. Any malt liquor.

**Oily** *adj.* A taste descriptor term used in the common parlance of whisky tasting. Defines any whisky falling into a group recognised as having heavier characteristics and otherwise described as woody, nutty, buttery and creamy.

**Olympics, Whisky** *n.* Tongue-in-cheek colloquialism, describing Scotland's annual week-long celebration of Gaelic language and culture. *Am Mòd Nàiseanta Rìoghail,* The Royal National Mod. As an event it is indeed similar to the Olympics, in that it moves its location in response to a successful competitive bid from a town or region. However, unlike the Olympics, brown envelopes are brazenly handed out in public, there is no drug testing, and performers tend to get better as they get older.

**Oom** (also **Owme**) *n.* (Scots) The visible vapours arising from the mash. Any steam or mist arising emitting from a vessel heating a liquid such as a kettle. Condensation.

**Optic** *n.* The small measuring chamber mounted onto a bar gantry. This transparent vessel fixed to the neck of an upturned bottle uses gravity to deliver an exact measure of spirit into a glass. Optics allow spirit to be quickly and accurately dispensed from the gantry by upward pressure, opening the valve levers which releases a single measure into the glass below. In Scotland, optics are traditionally sized to serve a quarter gill. In England they served a fifth or sixth of a gill until metrication in 1985 replaced these measures with 25ml and 35ml. To cater for the use of optics, all whisky producers produce and supply an upside-down label version of their popular brands and labelled bottles. These are designed to ensure the customer can easily identify their favourite brand, even when upside down.

## Output

**Output** *n.* The quantity of whisky produced by a distillery in any year. Output is measured in both gallons and litres per annum. Once this figure is known for each distillery, it can be used to project the volume of whisky produced within any group of distilleries, region, or even in the whole of Scotland in any one year. Indeed, the contribution of Scotch whisky as a whole to the UK Exchequer and the UK's GDP can easily be calculated by the total litres of whisky produced per year multiplied by the level of duty, currently 76%, on the price of each litre of whisky sold. The government strives to use this income produced entirely in Scotland wisely, for the health and welfare of the British people (who mostly live in England). On the other hand, Scotland can forever claim to produce the world's most intoxicating fresh air. At any time, we have twenty million filled whisky casks stored across the country. One per cent of this carefully crafted, maturing whisky simply evaporates each year in the **Angels' Share**.

PAGODA

MADE IN CHINA

# P

**Paddle** *n.* (Scots) Long-handled wooden tool with perforated paddle end, used in traditional mashing. The paddle was designed to enable the mashman to manually stir and mix the barley mash while also breaking up any clusters of the grist flour forming in the mix. Paddles were once the ubiquitous tools of whisky-making in the era of open-topped cast iron mashing vats. The arrival in the 1970s of the stainless steel enclosed lautering mashtuns ended the era of wooden paddles and they survive purely as an attractive piece of distillery decoration or collector's item of whisky distillery memorabilia.

**Pagoda roofs** *n.* As the railway network grew in the late 19th century, so larger distilleries were built in numbers along the rail routes in the remote rural areas where land was cheap. Key features of the production plant layout of these industrial distilleries were the malting kilns. These were built along the same lines as oatmeal mills and, especially in the highlands, fuelled by easily accessible peat. This use of peat to kiln the barley malt meant the *peat reek* or aroma hung in the air. This produced an intense peat reek flavouring which carried through into the whisky. As demand for whisky for blending grew in the 19th century, so did the demand for lighter, less intensely peaty whisky flavours to add to the blend. Innovative modifications in kiln design arrived in the 1890s which vented the peat reek through the roof to the outside air. These new kilns were characterised by distinctive high walls, steep pitched roofs and those louvred pagoda towers. These are the instantly recognisable, if now redundant, features of many Highland distilleries.

**Papin** *n.* (Scots) A traditional rural beverage made with a mixture of whisky, weak porridgey beer and oatmeal.

**Paralytic** *adj.* (Scots) The state of being rendered immobile, incommunicative and intensely burdensome to the company due to consumption of an excess of alcohol.

**Parting Glass (The)** *n.* The tradition of ensuring a visitor partakes of a final farewell glass or *deoch aig an dorus* (Scots Gaelic meaning 'drink at the door') before departing the company at the end of a convivial evening. Famously evoked in the song whose earliest version is recorded in the 17th century collection of Scottish airs, the *Skene Manuscript*. This lyric fragment is a portion of the poem known as 'Armstrong's Goodnight', a verse poignantly written in 1600 as a final farewell by one of the famous Border reiving Armstrong family before his execution for the murder of Sir John Carmichael, Warden and law keeper of the Scottish West March border land between Scotland and England. Today still a favourite of folk singers across the world, an original fragment is preserved in these lyrics:

> O, all the money e'er I had,
> I spent it in good company.
> And all the harm that ever I've done,
> alas it was to none but me.
> And all I've done for want of wit
> to mem'ry now I can't recall;
> So fill to me the parting glass,
> Good night and joy be with you all.
>
> O, all the comrades e'er I had,
> They're sorry for my going away.
> And all the sweethearts e'er I had,
> They'd wished me one more day to stay.

But since it falls unto my lot,
That I should rise and you should not,
I gently rise and softly call,
Goodnight and joy be with you all.

If I had money enough to spend,
And leisure time to sit awhile.
There is a fair maid in this town,
That sorely has my heart beguiled.
Her rosy cheeks and ruby lips,
I own, she has my heart in thrall;
Then fill to me the parting glass,
Good night and joy be with you all.

**Patent Still** *n.* The invention of the Patent still in Scotland in the 1820s enabled the continuous, cheap production of grain spirit, as opposed to the limited, more expensive batch production of the pot still method. Perfected by the Irish Exciseman-turned-distiller Aeneas **Coffey**, this method of distilling could produce whisky in a continuous process on an industrial scale. Also known as the Coffey still, this method uses two vertical columns in a continuous flowing process. Internally, perforated copper plates divide the columns horizontally into chambers. The process begins with dissolving the starch in unmalted cereals such as maize and wheat, by cooking in converters under steam pressure. This is mixed with a 10-15% measure of malted barley containing the natural enzymes that convert the starch into fermentable sugars. When yeast is added, the sugars ferment to create an alcoholic liquor of around 8% ABV. This liquor is sent to the first column, the Analyser, to be converted to hot spirit vapour (HSV). The HSV is then sent to the second column, the Rectifier. Here the heavier feints fall to the bottom while the refined spirit condenses near the top against cold wash pipes. Grain spirit distilled by this method is usually run off at around 94.0% ABV. It is then diluted usually to around 64% ABV before being filled into oak casks for its three years of maturation.

**Pattison crash** *n.* Perhaps the greatest ever Scotch whisky business crash. In 1900 the Pattisons Highland Distillers company greatly over-valued itself against its banking commitments. The company ostentatiously over-spent on building grand new offices in Leith, but almost immediately bankruptcy hit with a £500,000 deficit. This not only affected the company but also had a huge impact on Pattisons' closely knit and interconnected chain of suppliers. To compound the collapse, this coincided with one of the regular cyclical boom and bust depressions which have afflicted the Scotch whisky industry over the centuries. The Pattison crash is reckoned to have prompted a forty-year period of failures and closures of distilleries and merchants.

**Peaser** *n.* (Scots) A bumper measure of whisky.

**Peat** *n.* Peat is the naturally occurring deep fibrous layer of sodden, degenerating vegetation, built up over thousands of years on the surface of moorland. It defines vast areas of bare landscape and bog across Scotland. Peat is traditionally cut, lifted, dried and harvested each summer in many areas of the Highlands and Islands to provide winter fuel. Peat is also unique in that it is one of the most important signature ingredients of Scotch whisky. For centuries it has been used as a fuel to feed the fires beneath the stills and it also provides a '*peat reek*' flavour to the malt when its smoke is wafted through the drying barley. In matured and finished whisky this comes through in the aroma and on the palate as the **phenolic** flavour notes. The peat flavour content of any whisky can be measured and expressed as a figure in the 'parts per million' (ppm) of peat found in the volume of any whisky measure. Most strongly associated with Highland and Island whiskies, peat is now used sparingly in very accurate and controlled stages to deliver a spectrum of peatiness ranging from very lightly peated to very heavily peated. A lightly peated whisky might lie in the 1-10 ppm range whilst Bruichladdich's '**Octomore**', claimed to be the most heavily peated whisky in the world, boasts a mighty 208 ppm in its strongest expression.

**Peat-brew** *n.* (Scots) Colloquial name for Highland Whisky. Also, **Peat-bree**

**Peat-house** *n.* The building designated for dry storage and sorting of peat batches in a traditional distillery.

**Peat reek** *n.* (Scots) Smouldering peat gives off the highly distinctive and aromatic smoke which flavours the kilning barley. In the Highlands, whisky was traditionally made using peat-fired stills and kilns. In modern times, whisky makers have learned to 'control' peat smoke to deliver a measured peaty flavour infused into their malt barley. This is particularly true in the distilleries of Islay and Orkney whose whiskies profile peat as a signature aroma and taste on the nose and in the finish.

**Peckman** *n.* (Scots) The name given to a smuggler who transports illicit whisky across the country on horseback in a vessel shaped to look like a dried goods peck sack.

**Penny-wabble** *n.* (Scots) A weak or watery spirit, sold at a penny a bottle.

**Permitted Place** *n.* Under the Scotch Whisky Regulations, maturation of Scotch whisky must only be undertaken at *permitted places*. These places are specified as *'warehouses or premises in Scotland regulated by Her Majesty's Revenue and Customs (HMRC)'*. Any spirit not matured in a permitted place cannot be certified as Scotch whisky.

# Phenol

**Phenol** *n.* The flavour compound taken on by malt kilned using peat smoke and which carries through as a characteristic of the finished whisky. The intensity of this peat flavour is expressed as a trace measurement of parts per million (ppm) of the spirit sample. Lightly peated whisky generally lies in the 1-10 ppm range. Heavily peated malts kilned directly in the peat reek such as those from Islay contain phenolic traces as high as 100 ppm.

**Phenolic** *adj.* Describes the distinctive flavour of whisky distilled using peated malt. Phenolic whiskies are also often referred to as *smoky, carbolic, TCP, iodine, sea salt* and *kelpy*. These are most strongly associated with the range of single malt whiskies produced in the islands and, in particular, Islay. Peated malt is also used in other regions such as Highland and Speyside to produce phenolic variations of distillery's signature malt whiskies.

**Phenylalanine** *n.* In fermentation of the wort, phenylalanine is one of the group of slowly absorbed amino acids. These include *alanine, glycine, tryptophan* and *tyrosine*. Characteristically synthesised and absorbed late in fermentation by the yeast.

**Phylloxera** *n.* The microscopic insect we have to thank for the global popularity of Scotch whisky and the multibillion pound industry it sustains across the world. This alien invader was accidentally introduced to Europe in the 1850s by English botanists who collected specimens of American vines and brought them for transplanting in England. The *aphid nymphs* came with them, feeding on the vine roots, and soon the nascent English vineyards were infested and destroyed. An epidemic soon spread across the channel to France and French vineyards were similarly devastated. Somewhere between two-thirds and nine-tenths of European vineyards were destroyed and the production of wine and brandy crashed. However, the phylloxera mites had no interest in barley and whisky quickly replaced brandy as the spirit of choice across society. Scots distillers seized their opportunity and spent the next century expanding globally to establish Scotch whisky as the world's greatest spirit.

**Piece** *n.* (Scots) Traditional Scots name for a hogshead cask with a capacity of around 240 litres.

**Pigs** *n. pl.* On-site distillery piggeries and the keeping of other forms of livestock were popular as an efficient and rewarding means of disposing of draff and pot ale waste products. A herd of prime cattle were kept in the heart of the whisky capital of Glasgow, at Scotland's biggest 19th century distillery at Port Dundas.

**Pint-stoup** *n.* (Scots) A vessel for pouring a pint measure of liquor.

**Pipes** *n.* Coloured blue, red, black and white, pipes inside a distillery provide the visual key to the complexity of the process and what goes where as wort becomes wash, wash becomes low wines and low wines becomes spirit.

**Pipin-fou** *adj.* (Scots) Traditionally the piper at an event or a gathering is given a free and fulsome supply of whisky in return for providing the musical accompaniment. This gives rise to the phenomenon as the evening wears on that, despite having consumed plentifully and now unable to speak, the piper is still the embodiment of sobriety and skill when it comes to playing his pipes to the end of the evening. Thus the popular assertion that someone is *as drunk as a piper*.

**Pith** *n.* (Scots) Abbreviation for *pith of malt'*. Whisky.

**Plook** *n.* (Scots) The small knob or nipple marking the pour level at the top of a metal measuring vessel for dispensing spirits. Also, an inflamed pimple on the face.

# Póit

**Póit** *n.* (Gaeilge) A pot still. Also ironic name for a hangover.

**Poorie** *n.* (Scots) A small vessel for pouring liquor. A small quantity of liquor.

**Port** *n.* Port has a long connection with Scotland and the whisky trade. Its popularity arose in the late 18th century as tastes switched from Claret to Port fortified wine from Oporto in Portugal. Targeting the growing Scottish market and further afield, Scottish entrepreneurs moved to Portugal to become producers and today some famous sherry and port names bear testimony to their success. The Leith wine merchants, brothers John and Robert Cockburn, founded J and R Cockburn in 1815. Ayrshiremen James Duff and William Duff formed Duff-Gordon. William's relative Arthur Gordon established Bodegas Gordon. George Sandeman, from Perth, was in 1805 the first to fire-brand his casks, creating a recognisable distinctive trademark for his wines.

In the mid-1800s, the increasing popularity of these new sherries and ports meant growing stockpiles of used oak casks arriving steadily at the docks. This coincided with the Phylloxera mite devastation of the French brandy industry in the 1850s triggering increased demand for whisky. But the absence of commercially managed oak forestry meant there was huge demand for casks and so attention turned to the port and sherry cask stockpiles. Distillers soon realised that the port and sherry tones in the used oak casks added pleasant flavour characteristics to whisky. Thus the concept of finishing in port and sherry casks was born, and after two centuries this wonderful marriage of convenience is healthier than ever.

**Porter** *n.* A traditional dark style of beer also known as stout made from pale malt, baked in an oven or kiln until slightly browned.

**Port Pipe** *n.* A large cask at the top end of the limits for maturing Scotch whisky, the port pipe has a capacity of 650 litres. Distinctively thinner and taller than the more squat and rotund sherry butt which has a 500 litre capacity.

**Pot** *n.* (Scots) A small pot still. In Ireland, it is the root of the name *Poteen/Poitín*, the raw spirit produced in rural areas.

**Pot Ale** *n.* The oily residue left in the wash still after the first distillation. Pot ale is also known as *spent wash* and is passed through the heat exchanger to be recycled to start the next charge of wash in the still. It's reckoned that every litre of potable spirit made by distilleries produces at least nine litres of pot ale. The Scottish government's energy and recycling initiative Zero Waste Scotland has calculated that the industry produces 1.6 billion litres of pot ale and 500,000 tonnes of **draff** a year. Horizon Proteins, an enterprise spin-off from Heriot-Watt University in Edinburgh, has developed a process to use pot ale to create feed for Scottish salmon in fish farms, replacing soy and fishmeal normally imported from South America.

**Poteen** *n.* (Gaeilge **Poitín**) Name derived from the Gaeilge *Póit* meaning pot. The traditional, illicit Irish pot-distilled spirit or *mountain whiskey,* hand crafted and produced in small batches throughout Ireland. Can be produced from a wide range of *cereals, grain, whey, sugar beet, molasses* and even *potatoes*. Usually non-matured, its alcoholic strength can range between 40%- 90% ABV.

**Pot Stick** *n.* (Scots) A long-handled wooden stirring paddle or spirtle with vents to ensure an even and consistent mix of water and grist.

**Pot Still** *n.* Essentially a large copper kettle, the pot still is the key distilling vessel for transforming fermented 7-11% ABV alcoholic liquor into a clear refined spirit of 80% ABV. Scotch whisky production requires that pot stills should be made of copper. The interaction between the hot distilled vapours and the copper surface inside the still triggers chemical interactions which produce essential flavour elements. In most Scotch whisky production, the spirit batch is produced in a process involving two copper stills. Firstly, the wash is distilled in the Wash Still to produce a liquor of around 25% ABV called **Low Wines**. Then the Low Wines are distilled in the second, usually smaller Low Wines or Spirit Still to produce the new-make spirit at around 68-70% ABV. **Auchentoshan Distillery** is unique in Scotland for producing its whisky using a triple still distillation.

**Prestoune-ale** *n*. (Scots) Prestonpans beer.

**Prime** *v*. To deliberately intoxicate oneself or another with drink.

**Prohibition** *n*. The outright, nationwide, constitutional ban on alcohol in the United States that remained in place from 1920 to 1933. This tested the determination and ingenuity of the Scottish whisky producers trying to get back into growth and prosperity after the austerity of the First World War years. Prohibition imposed a ban on the production, importation, transportation and sale of alcoholic beverages. But loopholes existed and it proved possible to import small quantities of whisky into the States if designated as medicinal supplies. Illicit trade in the USA also took off on a significant scale and Scottish distillers could use pre-existing supply routes to the West Indies and Canada. Campbeltown distilleries, in particular, were especially active in securing links to the *bootleggers* and ensuring that demand was met, even if it meant quality was secondary. In January 1933 Franklin D Roosevelt was elected president with a pledge to repeal Prohibition, bringing this challenging era for the industry to an end.

**Proline** *n*. Proline and hydroxyproline are the two slowest absorbed amino acids in fermentation, lasting to the point where the yeast has exhausted the sugars in the wort and hence its growth capacity.

**Proof-barley** *n*. Barley that has been selected as perfect condition for malting.

**Protected Localities** *n*. Areas of Scotland with distinguishing whisky styles. The protected localities are; *Campbeltown*, comprising the South Kintyre ward of the Argyll and Bute Council as that ward is constituted in the Argyll and Bute (Electoral Arrangements) Order 2006, and *Islay*, comprising the Isle of Islay in Argyll. The definition *Island* is used to identify whiskies from the growing number of whisky producing islands which currently includes Islay, Jura, Skye, Arran, Mull, Lewis, Harris and Raasay.

**Protected Regions** *n*. These are the legally defined protected regions for whisky production. They are: **Highland**, comprising that part of Scotland that is north of the line dividing the Highland region from the Lowland region; **Lowland**, comprising that part of Scotland that is south of the line dividing the Highland region from the Lowland region; and **Speyside**, comprising the wards of Buckie, Elgin City North, Elgin City South, Fochabers, Lhanbryde, Forres, Heldon and Laich, Keith and Cullen and Speyside Glenlivet of the Moray Council. the island of **Islay**; and **Campbeltown**, comprising the South Kintyre ward of the Argyll and Bute Council.

**Puffer** *n*. The popular name for the small coal-fired, tramp steam-boats built in their hundreds to ply the west coast of Scotland in the first half of the 20th century. In Scotland, before post-war improvements to the road networks, the sea was the bulk transport route to remote communities up and down the west coast. The puffer fleets were essential for the whisky industry in key locations such as Campbeltown and Islay. Even today on Islay, the distilleries retain the purpose-built piers from the era of the puffers where the coal for the kilns could be offloaded and the finished whisky casks loaded. The Puffers were named after the characteristic rhythmic puffs of black smoke they produced from the coal-fired, single- screw engines. The early hull designs were squat and utilitarian, narrow enough to navigate the canal system but sufficiently robust to beach at low tide when delivering to islands without berthing facilities. Nearly twenty firms were involved in building these ships at yards along the Forth and Clyde Canal at Kirkintilloch and Maryhill.

**Puggy** *n.* (Scots) A drunk man.

**Puncheon** *n.* One of the standard sizes of casks selected for filling and finishing the spirit. Made from either American or European oak with a capacity of 500 litres, puncheons are characteristically squat and rotund looking casks when compared with the similar capacity of the taller Sherry butt.

**Put in the pin** *v.* (Scots) A colloquial expression meaning to give up strong drink. From the phrase *'to pit a pin in one's nose'*, meaning to put a stop to someone else's tomfoolery. To stop. To moderate. To control.

# Quaich

# Q

**Quaff** *n.* A draught of ale, beer or liquor. *v.* To drink enthusiastically.

**Quaich** *v. and n.* (Scots) From the Scots Gaelic **Cuach**. A traditional Scottish shallow drinking bowl. Usually a two-eared drinking cup or goblet made from wood, pewter and silver. Quaichs are typically bowl-shaped with a lipped handle on either side and can range from plain and functional to highly ornate and valuable. Traditionally used as a sharing vessel for passing round the company to mark friendship and ceremony. In Highland communities, the *Cuach Phòsta* or Wedding Quaich is filled and passed around after the marriage vows have been made to mark the beginning of the celebrations. Some members of the Scotch whisky industry have elevated the quaich to iconic status by forming the *Keepers of the Quaich*. The members of this exclusive, international, ceremonial, quasi-masonic, sort of Knights Templar-ish society meet annually to dress up and have splendid banquets in posh castles and palaces. And, of course, to *keep the quaich*.

**Quarter** *n.* With a capacity of around 80 litres, the quarter is one of the smallest casks used for maturing whisky. Its size means more whisky per litre contacts with the oak inner surface because of the greater ratio of surface area in direct contact with the contents. This creates a stronger, or more rapid interaction. The current trend for small-scale craft distilling has created renewed demand as these smaller casks age whisky more quickly.

# Queen

**Queen** *n.* (Scots) A stone grinding quern for milling cereal grains into grist for mashing.

**Quercus Alba** *n.* American white oak. One of the legally enshrined requirements for producing Scotch whisky is that it must be matured for three years in oak casks, crafted from either American white oak, *Quercus Alba* or European white oak, *Quercus Robur*. Japanese malts are matured in Mizunara or Japanese oak, *Quercus Mongolica*. Each is said to have different characteristics. American white oak grows faster and has a mellower, finer and more focused aroma to the Japanese or European oak. Japanese oak wood interacts with the spirit at a different rate and so needs more time to mature in the cask. Of the three types of oak used, American white oak wood is the fastest growing and can be cut down for cask making at around seventy years, while the slower growing European oak must be left for around 150 years.

**Quercus Mongolica** *n.* Mizunara or Japanese oak used in Japanese whisky production is said to have different characteristics from American or European oak. Japanese whiskies are often aged for longer as the flavour from the Japanese oak wood interacts with the spirit at a different rate and needs more time to mature in the cask.

**Quercus Robur** *n.* European white oak. The slower growing oak used in the first instance for making sherry and wine casks. It is reckoned that up to 70% of the character of the finished whisky is derived from its interaction with the wood as it lies in the cask.

**Quernie** *n.* (Scots) A grain of corn.

**Quickening** *n.* (Scots) The fermentation. Fermenting beer or ale that is added to pep up ale that has become flat or stale.

**Quill** *n.* (Scots) A bung or stopper for filling the bung hole in a cask.

**Quinkins** *n.* (Scots) The scum or dregs of any liquor leftovers.

# R

**Raffy** *adj.* (Scots) Drunken, ranting and loud.

**Raise** *v.* (Scots) To cause to ferment. To start a tune.

**Raisin-wine** *n.* (Scots) Traditional Scots name for French Brandy.

**Ramble** *n.* (Scots) A drinking bout. A spree. An unplanned drunken digression.

**Ramgeed** (also, **Ramjeed**) *adj.* (Scots) Being highly charged and fierce with intoxication. Furious with drink.

**Ramished** (also, **Rammist, Ramaged**) *adj.* (Scots) Confused with drink. Discombobulated or discomposed by alcohol.

**Randon** (also **Randan**) *n.* (Scots) A long and drunken carouse, a drunken revel.

**Raw** *n.* (Scots) New-made whisky straight from the still that has yet to be diluted.

**Reaming-fu** *adj.* (Scots) Overflowing. Over brimming.

**Red-shank** *n.* (Scots) A contemptuous name for a Highlander seen wearing the kilt in the Lowlands due to the exposed bare legs.

**Ree** (also **Reed**, **Reed-mad**) *adj.* (Scots) Excited with drink. Fiercely drunk. Wild with drink.

**Reek** *n.* (Scots) The distinctive intense smoky aroma from burning peat. Any overpowering smoky aroma from burning heaped organic matter. The *'Auld Reekie'* nickname for Edinburgh recalls the fog and stench of concentrated and uncontrollable smoke that wafted around the capital before its 19th century gentrification. Controlled exposure to peat reek in drying kilns imbues the smoky phenolic flavours into the barley that come through in the final spirit in a range from lightly peated to heavily peated.

**Reeky** *adj.* (Scots) Having a smoky or peaty flavour or aroma.

**Reel-rally** *adj.* (Scots) Staggering or unsteady under the influence of drink.

**Reflux** *n.* The usually bulbous-shaped feature on the head of pot stills. This feature of the still causes intense interactions between the hot rising vapours and the copper surface. The reflux shape, size and position on the still is unique to each distillery. Each reflux is designed to fit the still room and ensure peak interaction between the sulphide elements in the copper of the still and the superheated **ethanol** vapours before they pass through the lye arm to the condensers. Refluxes can be divided into three distinct still shapes: the **boil ball** still, lantern still and plain still. As the liquor is heated to boiling point in the body of the still, the rising flow of hot vapours enters the bowl of the reflux chamber. Here the flow becomes disrupted and vapour is recycled back into a hot maelstrom where it meets the copper still surface. It cools, condenses and falls back to be redistilled and vapourised again. The nature and intensity of the interactions within the reflux are also affected by the shape of the still and the angle of the **lye pipe**.

176

The impact on the flavour of the whisky is that the more intense the reflux interaction with the vapour, the lighter the taste notes to the spirit.

**Refresher** *n.* The first drink of the day. A single drink.

**Regions** *n.* There are five defined regions for Scotch whisky production, reflecting traditional craft variations. The Scotch Whisky Regulations 2009 describe these protected regions as: **Highland**, comprising that part of Scotland that is north of the line dividing the Highland region from the Lowland region; **Lowland**, comprising that part of Scotland that is south of the line dividing the Highland region from the Lowland region; **Speyside**, comprising the wards of Buckie, Elgin City North, Elgin City South, Fochabers, Lhanbryde, Forres, Heldon and Laich, Keith and Cullen and Speyside Glenlivet of the Moray Council; the island of **Islay**; and **Campbeltown**, comprising the South Kintyre ward of the Argyll and Bute Council.

**Rejuvenation** *n.* The process whereby a cask which has lain for between three and twenty years in a dark warehouse, slowly maturing the spirit within, is emptied, dried and renewed to its youthful condition. Once the bung has been removed and the whisky extracted, the cask is opened, dried and the dark, spirit-stained, inside layer scraped back to a surface of bright, fresh wood. The cask is now, to all extents and purposes, a new cask with all the maturation qualities of the oak available. By toasting in an oven and charring the inside, the wood cellulose is again fractured and sugar compounds converted to release the flavour and aromatic qualities of the wood. A bourbon cask, used for two to four years in the USA, can be used for another thirty in Scotland and might be refilled two, three or even four times before its maturation life is over. Then the spirit will have penetrated so deeply that the cask is judged to have lost its wood membrane integrity.

**Retort** *n*. The archaic, basic copper distilling vessel developed for use by the early alchemists and apothecaries. Its single vessel shape has often been compared to the curlew, goose or even pelican. Over time the basic design elements of the retort were improved and evolved into the more sophisticated and efficient two-vessel combination of copper still and attached condensers which come in a multitude of variations today from small home distilling kits to the vast still complexes sited on commercial distilleries.

**Reum** *n*. (Scots) The foaming froth on top of a fermenting wash.

**Riveted still** *n*. Riveting was the traditional method of fabricating copper stills until the more flexible and efficient method of soldering became the tried and tested method used by coppersmiths to seal the copper plates. Founded in 1790, Balblair on the Dornoch Firth was probably the last distillery in Scotland to have a riveted wash still in operational use.

**ROPP cap** *n*. Roll-on, Pilfer-Proof cap. The most common type of whisky bottle top, used mainly in the blend market. Familiar as the screw thread aluminium with the 'clicking' breakaway band. The malt market tends to prefer the cork and capsule bottle top.

**Rory** *adj*. (Scots) Roaring drunk.

**Ruber** *n*. (Scots) A wine or liquor cask.

**Rudder** *n*. (Scots) A wooden implement for stirring the brewing mash, also known as a *paddle*.

**Rummager** *n*. A feature of wash stills heated directly from below by coal or peat furnaces. This direct heat applied to the copper base can cause solids in the wash inside the still to burn onto the surface. If the heat continues to be applied this can increasingly taint the flavour of the batch with burnt flavour tones. The copper chained rummager was developed as a method of continuously stirring the wash at the base of the still during the boiling to prevent this.

**Run** *n*. The stage in distilling when a full charge of liquor is processed from start to finish by heating in wash still or spirit still to produce **ethanol** vapour condensed into firstly **low wines** or **new-make** spirit. A smuggling sea voyage or overland trek.

**Running-trade** *n*. (Scots) A genteel 18th century euphemism for smuggling, e.g. *He has substantial interests invested in the running-trade.* He's a smuggler.

**Run-off** *v*. To discharge a filled liquor vessel or pipe to another receiver. To fill.
  *n*. Leakage. Seepage.

**Rusty Nail** *n*. A simple whisky cocktail created in the 1930s which became popular in the 1960s amongst New York's glamorous hard-drinking Rat Pack scene. Made from a combination of Drambuie liqueur and neat whisky in measures graded to the taster's preference. The cocktail is also known as Smoky Nail whenever the distinctive flavour of a peaty malt whisky such as Laphroaig is used.

**Rye** *n*. Originating in Eastern Europe, rye is a grass cereal crop, similar to wheat and barley. It is particularly robust and grows well in the colder climates of Northern and Eastern Europe and in poorer soils. Now grown in most continents including North America it is the primary component of *Rye Whiskey* which, under United States law, must be made from a mash containing a minimum fifty-one per cent Rye grains.

**Rye Whiskey** *n*. Chiefly associated with North America, rye whiskey is a drier, lighter flavoured spirit than Bourbon, distilled by law from at least 51% rye grains. it is produced in both Canada and the United States. At one time rye whiskey was the predominant whiskey of choice and ubiquitous across the North-Eastern states. In the U.S. rye whiskey was badly hit by the **Prohibition** era and production in these states never recovered after its repeal in 1933. Since the turn of the 21$^{st}$ century there has been a renaissance of sorts in the production of rye whiskey with introduction of new brands on the back of the successful Bourbon industry based in the state of Kentucky.

Conversely, Canadian rye whisky has no legal requirement or measure placed on the amount of rye used in production of the spirit. This is largely because Canadian rye has evolved down the blended path. Over time the amount of rye used in the blend has reduced and cereals such as corn have increasingly become the core grain with rye being used minimally as flavouring. Exceptionally, there remain a couple of premium brands such as *Canadian Club* and *Alberta Premium* produced using 100% rye mash. Over time Canada's tastes have settled on a whisky that is a style of blend based more on corn spirit with a taste and aroma of rye, recognised as 'Canadian whisky'. These blends can be labelled as *Canadian Rye Whisky, Canadian Whisky or Rye Whisky*. However, Canadian Rye whisky cannot be sold in the United States as 'rye whisky'.

# S

**Saccharification** *n.* The process whereby the starch stored in dormant barley grains is converted to sugar. By controlled application and management of heat and moisture conditions during the malting and mashing processes, the grains are tricked into believing 'spring has sprung' triggering germination. Enzymes act on starch stored in the grain, making it accessible and soluble for conversion to sugars. This activates the diastase enzyme group, promoting the growth of shoots and roots, or **cuilms**. When the **maltman** reckons saccharification has reached its peak in the green malt the process is halted by air drying and draining. The low moisture high sugar content malted barley is now in prime condition for cooking or mashing.

**Saint Monday** *n.* (Scots) Traditional name for the day Scots working men would spend their wages on drink.

**Saladin Box** (also known as **Saladin Bin**) *n.* A 19th century French invention for steeping and germinating barley in a concrete trough with a perforated floor. The new Saladin approach advanced malting techniques and improved efficiency by pouring malting barley into the trough, to a depth of about four feet then blowing temperature controlled air through the perforations. Saladins were thereafter adopted across the industry as they maximised use of floor space in maltings by containing the barley in large rectangular boxes. There the malt could be consistently turned and dried using rotating spiral screws and the forced fan ventilation. Still widely used in malting today, this method ensures efficient steeping and germinating throughout large quantities and by consistent control of humidity and temperature. Saladin boxes are usually sized to handle between thirty and fifty tonnes of barley. When the malted grain is ready for the kiln it is pumped out of the Saladin box through hoses. Individual distilleries adopted and built their own Saladin malting halls, especially many north Highland distilleries after World War II. From the 1960s, malting barley became a specialist industry. Rather than malting their barley onsite, distillers found it more cost effective, convenient and efficient to use commercial maltsters. These large, specialist malting plants operate on industrial scales, using vast Steeping Germination and Kilning Vessels (SGKVs). In most distilleries Saladins have largely have been abandoned but are still used in malting plants.

**Sand-bed** *n.* (Scots) An inveterate drunkard or drunken layabout.

**Sap** *n.* (Scots) Any liquor that is served and drunk as an accompaniment to food.

**Sappy** *adj.* (Scots) Of wood, moist with resin. Saturated. Of a person, lively and gregarious through drinking liquor. Given to habitual drinking. Of kisses, full, plump, sweet.

**Sark** *n.* (Scots) A long shirt or chemise. A night shirt. Most famously referenced in the epic Robert Burns poem, 'Tam o' Shanter', as the scanty *cutty sark* slip worn by the wild and entrancing young witch *Nannie*.

> Her cutty sark, o' Paisley harn,
> That while a lassie she had worn,
> In longitude tho' sorely scanty,
> It was her best, and she was vauntie.
> Ah! little kend thy reverend grannie
> That sark she coft for her wee Nannie

> Wi' twa pund Scots ('twas a' her riches)
> Wad ever graced a dance of witches!

Tam becomes so aroused by the raw sexuality of Nannie's dancing that he forgets his perilous circumstance and yells out 'Weel done Cutty Sark!' In doing so he alerts the witches and demons and even Auld Nick (the Devil) himself to his presence. But in fleeing the chasing hellish horde Tam sacrifices his faithful horse Meg's tail to Nannie's outstretched hand just as they clear the keystone on the Doon Bridge. Cutty Sark nowadays is famously the name of the preserved tea clipper ship at Greenwich. It is also one of the world's best known whisky brands. Cutty Sark has been one of Scotland's most popular blends for over 90 years with its recipe of specially selected whiskies producing a light, vibrant colour and mellow flavour, ideal for mixing and cocktails.

**Scaddit-ale** n. (Scots) A drink made with hot ale or beer mixed with a little meal or oats to create a warm, gloopy, alcoholic gruel.

**Scaddit-wine** n. (Scots) A warmed or mulled wine.

**Scalch** n. (Scots) A large morning dram. From the Scots Gaelic word *sgailc* meaning 'a blow to the head' or skelp.

**Scoll** v. (Scots) To drink to one's health, to toast the company before sharing a drink. From the Scandinavian drinking toast *'Skål'*.

**Scoop** n. (Scots) A wooden drinking cup. A cap. A draught of liquor taken enthusiastically as in *'D'ye fancy a few scoops an' a Ruby Murray?'*

**Scoor** n. A big draught of liquor. A swallowed dose of liquor or medication.
>       v. (Scots) To clear out. To scrape down to the bottom.

Scoor-the-gate

**Scoor-the-gate** *n*. (Scots) An ale or liquor that causes diarrhoea.

**Scoot** (also **Scootie**, **Scuit**, **Scute**) *n*. (Scots) A wooden drinking vessel.

**Scootie-fu** *adj*. (Scots) A full measure of liquor from a filled *scootie* or drinking cup.

**Scootiken** *n*. (Scots) A small dram of whisky.

**Scotch** *n*. The single word that has travelled around the globe, infiltrated every culture it has encountered and entered every nation's language to mean *whisky*. Everywhere except, of course, Scotland. Shorthand for *'Scotch whisky'*, the word *Scotch* is never used in Scotland to accurately describe anything of Scotland or from Scotland. Any usage by a Scot tends to be reserved for deliberate ironic effect when caricaturing an English or American perspective on anything Scottish. Across the world its single syllable and simple sibilant and glottal brevity makes its easily vocable in any language. Thus over the centuries it has come to be absorbed into such diverse languages as Arabic, Bangla, Croatian, Dutch, Esperanto, French, Greek, Hindi, Italian, Japanese, Korean, Latvian, Mongolian, Norwegian, Polish, Russian, Swahili, Turkish, Ukrainian, Vietnamese, Welsh, Xhosa, Yiddish and Zulu.

**Scotch-convoy** (also **Scots-convoy**) *n*. (Scots) A traditional, rural custom of thanking one's visitor/s at the end of an evening of convivial company and ceilidh-ing. This is expressed by escorting the visitor all the way back to their own home where, on arrival at the visitor's home, the roles of visitor and host are reversed and a drink offered. Often this triggers an extension of the evening of convivial company into the wee small hours requiring further back-and-fro *Scotch-convoying* until fatigue or morning chores necessitates rest and a break in the conviviality.

**Scotch mist** *n.* Characteristically soft precipitation unique to Scotland. Microscopic, invisible, gravity-defying rain that hangs in the air like smoke but quietly soaks through all forms of clothing.

**Scotch Whisky Association** *n.* The internationally recognised representative body for Scotland's whisky industry and all its constituent parts, from malting floors to international auction rooms. The SWA originated in 1912 with the creation of the Wine and Spirit Brand Association. This body came into being in response to Chancellor Lloyd George's raising of taxes from alcohol to pay for his programme of social reforms. His tax on whisky rose by 30% in 1909, causing sales to crash and panic across the industry. In an effort to bolster their brands, owners held a major gathering in London on 3 October 1912, and the outcome was an agreement to set-up the Wine & Spirit Brand Association.

War dominated the Association's early history, as during World War I, the new body opposed Lloyd George's threat of prohibition and state control of the trade. Such debates made it clear that a strong body focused on whisky alone was needed and, in 1917, the organisation changed its name to the Whisky Association, covering both Scottish and Irish producers. During World War II the fundamental issue was whether whisky could be made at a time of rationing. The government argued that because the country was bankrupt and needed to earn more currency overseas, cereals would only be released if companies agreed to export more. One Minister said: 'the country needs food, dollars mean food, and whisky means dollars.'

The Scotch Whisky Association, as it was renamed in 1942, spent the best part of the next decade arguing that it was in the national interest to allow distillers to use scarce cereals, and won the argument. From 23 November 2009, the Scotch Whisky Regulations 2009 legally defined the product Scotch whisky. These regulations govern the production, labelling, packaging and advertising of Scotch whisky in the United Kingdom and form the basis for the legal protection of Scotch whisky as a global product and a global industry.

**Scottish Craft Distillers Association (SCDA)** *n.* Formed in 2014 to accommodate the rapid emergence of craft distillers and small scale distillery projects across Scotland. The SCDA now has over 30 members representing producers of spirits including whisky, gin, vodka, rum, calvados and liqueurs.

**Scout** *n.* (Scots) A small, beamy open sailing boat named after the Scots word for a razorbill or guillemot, popular for inshore smuggling runs.

*v.* To squirt, spurt or eject liquid forcibly from a spout.

**Scow** *n.* (Scots) In coopering or cask making, a barrel stave, a wooden plank from which a barrel stave is made. The outside board taken from a felled tree.

*v.* In coopering or cask-making, to knock in staves. To trim staves or wood.

**Scowff** *v.* (Scots) To swallow or down a drink in a single draught.

**Seefer** *n.* (Scots) A drunken worthless layabout or loafer.

**Seep** *v.* (Scots) To ooze, leak. To percolate. In drinking, to drain the dregs.

**Seepage** *n.* (Scots) The leakage of spirit through the cask seals.

**Settlins** *n.* (Scots) Sediment. The dregs left in the bottom of a vessel, vat or bottle.

**Set to** *v.* (Scots) In a tasting, to address the task in hand. To begin.

**Sgalc-nid** *n*. (Scots Gaelic *Skaalk+Neet*) Traditionally the first of four ceremonial drams dispensed in the household as the menfolk prepare on the morning of days of great emotional significance such as weddings and funerals. Literally translates as *the dram of the nest*. In reality a generous measure of whisky enjoyed in the morning whilst still reclining in bed.

**SGKV** *n*. Acronym for the multi-purpose Steeping, Germination, Kilning Vessels (SGKVs) used in industrial scale malting plants. These huge stainless steel drums have the capacity to process between 100 and 350 tonnes of malt at one time, from initial steeping through to final kilning. The perforated, rotating steel floors and internal combs of ribbon turners enable very large quantities of barley to be sequentially steeped, drained, turned, sifted and finally kilned. SGKVs produce and maintain the key conditions required for malting while containing and handling barley on a vast scale. This takes place over four to six days and requires a continuous supply and drainage of water and temperature controlled air venting, enabling the maltsters to soak and dry large quantities of barley whilst ensuring consistent control of moisture content.

**Shallow still** *n*. Also known as the *Lowland* or *Millar* still. The Lowland still was pan-shaped, wide and shallow. The design enabled it to run spirit extremely fast and often, thus circumventing 19th century government licence restrictions and regulations. The wash filled the pan just a few inches deep and usually just about over the minimum legal capacity. The still's heated coils forced the evaporation. Lowland stills could run a batch of spirit in three minutes, delivering huge efficiency gains over the larger pot still. With no reflux ball the spirit the Lowland produced was fiery and much coarser than the Highland or pot still requiring it to be rectified or spiced. The crown intervened to prohibit all stills under 2000 gallons in 1814.

**Shell** *n*. The outer husk of the barley grain.

## Sherry

**Sherry** *n.* Wine made from white grapes then fortified with wine spirit to increase its alcohol content. Regionally protected to the region of Andalusia in northern Spain, sherry ranges in style from light, young wines drunk to accompany meals to darker and heavier oak aged styles such as Oloroso and Amontillado with an alcohol content of at least 17% ABV. For over 200 years, whisky makers have used the special qualities of matured fortified wines, especially sherry, to add colour and flavour. These flavour tones are brigaded in two groups based on the type of oak cask. European oak produces notes of dried fruits, tannin, resin and cloves. American oak produces coconut, spice, vanilla and chocolate notes. Even without the link to whisky, sherry and port have long continuous historical connections with Scotland, through the trade routes between the continent and Leith.

Sherry is first recorded as being drunk in Edinburgh in 1548, and its popularity soon permeated through the mercantile classes. Recognising opportunities in the growing market, Scots entrepreneurs set out to become producers in Spain and Portugal and today some famous sherry and port names bear testimony to their success. The Leith wine merchant brothers John and Robert Cockburn founded J and R Cockburn in 1815. Ayrshiremen James and William Duff formed Duff-Gordon, William's relative Arthur Gordon established Bodegas Gordon, and George Sandeman from Perth, who in 1805 was the first to fire-brand his casks, created with his name a recognisable distinctive trademark. A seventh-generation George Sandeman is still with the company. In the mid-1800s, the growing popularity of these new sherries and ports being shipped to Glasgow, Perth and Leith meant increasing stock-piling of used oak casks, coinciding with the **Phylloxera** mite devastation of the French Brandy industry in 1863 and subsequent increased demand in England for whisky. The lack of commercially managed oak forestry in Scotland meant there was a huge demand for oak casks, but distillers realised that a ready supply was steadily arriving at the docks. They soon realised the sherry tones added flavour characteristics to the whisky. So, the concept of finishing in sherry casks was born and after two centuries this wonderful marriage of convenience is healthier than ever and celebrated across the world.

**Sherry Butt** *n*. One of the standard sizes of casks selected for filling and finishing the spirit. Made from European oak with a capacity of 500 litres, sherry butts are characteristically taller and narrower than the larger capacity, dumpier Sherry puncheon.

**Sherry Puncheon** *n*. One of the largest capacity liquor transport or storage casks. This 667-litre monster is at the upper limit of oak cask size allowed for maturing Scotch whisky.

**Shot** *n*. (Scots) Strong whisky. *Going on the shot* is purposely setting out on a drinking binge of strong whisky or spirit with the sole intention of experiencing a sustained, indeterminate period of alcoholic inebriation.

**Shyrie** *adj*. (Scots) Thin and watery, used in description of any liquor.

**Silent Season** *n*. At some point in the year every distillery closes its doors and stops production for days, or even weeks, of maintenance, deep cleaning, testing of all processes and renewal of any materials reaching the end of useful life. Called the silent season, this time is also known as the *Holidays*, when distillery workers give their senses a rest from constant immersion in the rich, aromatic air of the distillery. For some it can be a long two weeks and the chance to travel, sampling other country's spirits and liqueurs, only makes them hanker for a return to the warm, familiar sights and smells of their home distillery.

**Sind** (also **Synde**) *v*. (Scots) To wash down food with a drink. To rinse, to quench.

## Single Grain

**Single Grain** *n*. Defined in the Scotch Whisky regulations as 'Scotch Whisky which in addition to water and malted barley, has been produced from whole grains of other malted or unmalted cereals and distilled at a single distillery.' Excluded from the definition of Single Grain Scotch Whisky is any spirit which qualifies as a Single Malt Scotch Whisky or as a Blended Scotch Whisky. The latter exclusion is to ensure that a Blended Scotch Whisky produced from Single Malt and Single Grain distilled at the same distillery does not also qualify as Single Grain Scotch Whisky.

**Single Malt** *n*. Defined in the Scotch Whisky Regulations as 'a Scotch Whisky produced from only water and malted barley at a single distillery by batch distillation in pot stills.' It is illegal to export single malt Scotch Whisky in any form other than a bottle labelled for retail sale.

**Sip** *v*. To use the lips while drinking liquor to control the measure taken and ensure only a small amount passes into the mouth.
    *n*. A miniscule measure. In whisky tasting the contact made between lips and the spirit to enable a small sample to be analysed on the palate.

**Siping** *n. pl. and adj.* (Scots) Oozings, leaks from a failing cask. Soaking. Of a cask, leaky, seeping.

**Sipit** *adj*. (Scots) Dried up. Drained of moisture.

**Sipple** *v. and n.* (Scots) To sip continuously. To tipple. A tipple. Also, **Sippler**. One who tipples continuously.

**Sitting-drink** *n*. (Scots) A drink taken in company for a period of long duration.

**Skalk** *n*. (Scots) From Scots Gaelic *Sgailc*. The occasional Highland indulgence of enjoying whisky for breakfast. In Gaelic, its primary meaning is a blow to the head. This has understandably lent its meaning to describe a large, generous measure of whisky taken in the morning. This practice is perfectly acceptable if reserved for very particular circumstances and special days such as noted in 1783 by Dr Samuel Johnson during his Tour to the Hebrides:

> 'A man of the Hebrides, for of the woman's diet I can give no account, as soon as he appears in the morning, swallows a glass of whisky; yet they are not a drunken race, at least I never was present at much intemperance; but no man is so abstemious as to refuse the morning dram, which they call a skalk.'

Also known as the morning bumper.

**Skeil** *n.* (Scots) A wooden drinking vessel with a handle.

**Skink** (also **Skynk**) *n.* (Scots) A drinking bout. A rich broth made from a mixture of mashed vegetables and meat or fish.
    *v.* To drink a toast in ratification of a bargain or agreement. To charge glasses with drink, to pour out a measure. To decant, serve with drink. To tipple.

**Skinker** *n.* (Scots) Someone who serves drink. A butler. A tippler. A drinker.

**Skole** (also **Skolt**) *v.* (Scots) To drink hard, to salute with drink, to toast health with drink.

**Skoot** *n.* (Scots) Sour, dead or flat liquor.

**Skouff** *v.* (Scots) To quaff or drink off.

**Skutie** *n.* (Scots) A wooden drinking vessel.

**Slack**

**Slack** *v.* (Scots) To quench the thirst, to slake.

**Slaps** *n.* (Scots) Liquor of poor quality.

**Sleeping Distillery** *n.* Describes a distillery which although not in operation still retains intact the necessary buildings, infrastructure and potential for services to enable it to resume production.

**Sloat** *v.* To drink heartily and plentifully.
   *n.* (Scots) A voracious and hearty drinker. A notoriously enthusiastic boozer.

**Slock** *v. and n.* (Scots) To slake the thirst. Any intoxicating drink.

**Slockener** *n.* (Scots) Any thirst quenching drink.

**Slok** *v.* (Scots) To spend money on alcoholic drink.

**Slug** (also **Sluggy**) *v.* To swallow a full measure of drink greedily.
   *n.* (Scots) One who drinks continuously but never seems to appear drunk as in: *He's a slug with the drink*.

**Sma' Still** *n.* (Scots) The small single copper stills used in the 18th and 19th centuries throughout the Highlands and rural Scotland to produced small batch illicit whisky. The size of these stills made them mobile and easily hidden both in operation and in transit.

**Smeller** *n.* (Scots) A small sample of spirits or liquor.

**Smick** *n.* (Scots) A spot or tincture of spirit.

**Sneck** *v.* (Scots) To drink off. To drink to the finish.

**Sniff** *v.* To inhale through the nose for the purposes of forensic examination of an odour or aroma, for identifying its elemental ingredients, especially in whisky tastings.

*n.* The all-important first encounter between the **nose** and the whisky vapour after the bottle is uncorked and the whisky poured into the glass. To ensure maximum detail in sampling the aroma the nose should be fully inserted within the neck of the glass with mouth slightly open to ensure maximum aroma circulation. Thereafter the sniff should be drawn in by a slow, shallow inhale through the nostrils and mouth to the back of the throat.

**Snuittit** *adj.* (Scots) Having a dazed look. Appearing half-drunk, stupid.

**Sobersides** *n.* (Scots) Someone known to be of sober, alcohol-averse drinking habits or repute.

**Solera** *n.* The blending technique originating in Spain and Portugal. Solera manages consistency of taste and quality of product and therefore a brand over time. This is done by blending new make wines with older vintage wines held in bodegas in casks to advance maturity and flavour. Over the years this topping-up of casks with older vintages increases the average age of the finished contents. Solera is used in the production of port, sherry, madeira and marsala as well as brandy, beer, rums, sherry vinegars. Glenfiddich use the technique for their Solera expression.

**Sonsy-folk** *n.* (Scots) The collective name for the tradition of first foot visitors to a house on New Year's Day. Regarded as bringing good luck.

**Sooch** *v.* To swill, to swig off a full measure.
*n.* (Scots) A copious large draught or measure of ale or liquor.

**Sook** *v.* (Scots) To drink slowly and leisurely. To sip a glass.

**Soup, Sowp** *v.* (Scots) To sup or tipple.

**Sour Mash** *n.* A process in Bourbon whiskey distilling. The sour mash involves adding acidic residue or *'backset'* from the previous spirit distillation to the early stages of the next process. This might happen in the grain mashing or in the fermentation, or both. The purpose of sour mash is to lower the pH and inhibit the activity of wild yeast and any bacteria present.

**Sowk** *v.* (Scots) To drench or overfill.

**Spa** *n.* (Scots) Any alcoholic drink or liquor.

**Spairge** (also **Sporage**) *v.* (Scots) To sprinkle.

**Sparge** *v. and n.* The final flush or charge of water through the mash tun at the end of the mashing of a batch. Heated at about 85°C this final run dissolves the last of the sugars in the solids left in the base of the mash tun. This liquid is drained off to be used as the first charge of water in the next batch of grist at the start of the next mash cycle at a controlled temperature of 64°C.

**Spark** *n.* (Scots) A nip. A small drop of whisky or quantity of liquor, '*a spark in the house*' is a saying meaning a craving for a drink.

**Spent lees** *n.* The residue left in the spirit still, unusable for spirit after the second distillation. As much as 40% of the 10,000 litres of low wines distilled in the second distillation is rejected as spent lees. This rich, oily liquor is disposed of in various ways, depending on the size and location of the distillery. It may be naturally recycled on site through evaporation in specially created reed drainage beds or ponds or, otherwise, uplifted by tankers to be diluted and recycled as sprayed agricultural fertiliser. Island distilleries are permitted to flush lees directly into the sea through long outfalls.

**Spewing-fou** *adj.* (Scots) Drunk to sickness. Paralytic.

**Spink** *adj.* (Scots) Of ale, of good quality.

**Spinkie** *n.* (Scots) A small dram or glass of spirits.

**Speyside** *n.* One of the **protected regions** defined in the Scotch Whisky Regulations. The traditional Scots name is Strathspey, derived from the Scots Gaelic *Srath Spè*. Malt whiskies are from the *strath*, or valley plain, of the river Spey. Almost half of Scotland's malt distilleries are located in the Speyside protected region, reflecting the area's status as the country's heartland of fine whisky production. Tasting notes are characteristically smooth, succulent, sherried notes with a sweet or dry finish. Speyside comprises the wards of Buckie, Elgin City North, Elgin City South, Fochabers, Lhanbryde, Forres, Heldon and Laich, Keith and Cullen and Speyside Glenlivet of the Moray Council and the Badenoch and Strathspey ward of the Highland Council.

**Spinnle** *v.* (Scots) To malt. To grow roots and shoots in grains of barley.

**Spirit** *n.* Spirit is defined as the product of a distillation, usually occurring in an alembic chamber. Spirit can be distilled from a range of organic materials and generally describes the liquid-condensed vapours of the process. Distillates are produced by using heat to vaporise alcoholic liquids which are condensed as spirit. Spirits, even those for drinking, tend to be volatile and flammable and those produced in this way for drinking are defined as 'potable spirit'. Whisky spirit is produced by distilling the sugars or saccharified materials released from cooked or mashed cereals such as maize, wheat or malted barley.

**Spirit Safe** *n.* The imposing padlock-sealed box or casket of brass and glass inside any still house through which the new-make spirit flows. The spirit safe was introduced by law in 1823 by Customs and Excise to ensure HM government had absolute oversight and control of the finished distilled spirit. In each distillery the device was positioned centrally and prominently in the still house at the outrun of the pot still. The spirit safe was one of a raft of legal measures to ensure scrutiny and government control over spirit production and revenue dues. A resident **Excise Officer** was posted to each distillery to monitor all production. He literally had the keys and the powers to lock the spirit safe and bonded warehouses, enabling him to record exactly the amount of taxable spirit produced in each distillery and where it was.

**Spirit Still** *n*. Sometimes called the **Low Wines** still, the spirit still is where the second distillation takes place. It is often a third smaller than the wash still. In the spirit run, the spirit still is charged with the low wines liquor produced by the wash distillation, at around 25% ABV, and is combined with the **foreshots** and **feints** from the previous distillation. As the liquor reaches boiling point the alcohol evaporates and travels up the neck of the still into the dynamic vortex of the reflux. Here complex flavouring compounds (**congeners**) form as the vapour interacts with the copper surface. The vapour continues its journey up through the still until it passes over the lyne arm and down into the condenser. Here it meets the cold copper and cools to form a liquid spirit of around 80-90% ABV. This final distillate now passes through the spirit safe as a clear, colourless spirit. The stillman makes a judgement on when to separate it into its three distinct parts: the foreshots, the heart, and the feints, also described as heads, heart, and tails. The cut-off point for each fraction is peculiar to each distillery and has a significant effect on character and quality.

**Spleut** *n*. (Scots) A splash.

**Spleutter** *v*. (Scots) To spill clumsily, or awkwardly when pouring. To ruin a drink with a heavy splash or a clumsy *spleut*.

**Spootragh** *n*. (Scots) An alcoholic drink of any kind.

**Spreading-drink** *n*. (Scots) An old trade custom of sharing a drink on reaching an agreement.

**Spree** *n*. (Scots) A boisterous sally forth by a company of lads or lassies out for an extended tour of all the local taverns and public houses in the pursuit of good drink and good craic. A noisy, riotous, but good-natured drinking bout or adventure.

**Spuny** *v*. To broach or tap a cask of whisky or wine, to draw out whisky from a cask.
    *n*. (Scots) A heavy blow

**Stable-meal** *n*. (Scots) Liquor provided at a stabling inn to drovers and other travellers overnighting their horses.

**Staile** *n*. (Scots Gaelic, *Staal'yeh*) A Highland still. Local distilling was a commonplace and entirely natural activity throughout the Gaelic-speaking Highlands, Islands and rural Scotland up to the mid-1800s. Such was the popularity and volume of the spirit produced that the name *whisky*, derived from lowland pronunciation of the Gaelic *Uisge Beatha*, was adopted as the universal generic name for Scotland's 'water of life'.

**Standing-drink** *n*. (Scots) An alcoholic drink taken hastily, while standing.

**Stap** *v*. *'To fa' a' staps'* To fall all to pieces. Also **Step.**
    *n*. (Scots) A single stave of a cask or tub.

**Starlaw** – see **Grain distilleries**

**Stave** *n*. Long, narrow bowed slats of oak wood tapered along their length. Used vertically as the building planks for whisky casks these are much more expensive than an ordinary piece of timber.

The cut selected from the tree is angled to minimise the effect of radial xylem vessels leading from the core of the trunk to the bark. Since these would make the staves leaky, the trunk must be cut in special patterns such as star cut, mirror cut and rift cut with the annual rings running vertically. The method is wasteful in that a great deal of the cut log goes unused. Once cut, the stave is dried to a maximum 10% residual moisture. The craft of the cooper is to ensure the staves butt exactly to each other on either side of the reed seal, when the pressure of galvanised iron hoops ensures a perfectly sealed cask. Standard staves are generally around 88 cm long, about 2.5 cm thick and are of various widths. Transport quality casks are thicker and more robust at 2.7 cm.

**Steam** *n*. The 'ghost in the machine' in whisky production. Steam might be invisible but it plays a huge part in the process of making Scotch whisky. Before the advent of the steam age pot stills were traditionally heated directly from beneath, using peat, coal, anthracite or, in the case of illicit distilling out in the hills, smokeless juniper wood. Steam arrived in whisky production in the late 18th century, firstly in the form of direct steam heat onto the copper surface of the pot still. The efficiency of this method was improved with the design of metal cavity steam chambers or jackets around the still. This was further improved with the introduction of indirect heating by steam coils then direct heating of the wash with steam coils inside the pot still.

**Steam coil** *n*. In pot still distillation, the method of channelling of superheated steam heat directly to the wash by way of stainless steel coils around the interior base of the pot stills.

**Steam Jacket** *n*. A method of heating a mashing vessel by enclosing it within a steel jacket with a cavity for circulating superheated steam around it.

**Steep** *v.* The simple process of soaking the barley grains in warm water until the saturated grains are tricked into germination. This causes the grain to swell in size, produce starch and chit roots and shoots.

**Still** *n.* Essentially a large copper kettle. A still is the simple vessel and apparatus which comprises the oldest and most basic method for distilling quantities of spirit. Evolved from ancient onion-shaped, **alembic vessels** comprising a liquor-filled copper chamber shaped to taper in a cap at the top and heated from below. This neck narrows to feed the rising hot vapour out via a pipe to condense as a liquid in a water-cooled collecting chamber. This design has been adapted over the centuries for increased industrial scale production. In Scotch whisky production this has produced variations of stills to deliver spirit production efficiency, potency, taste and speed. These variations include the *pot still, pan still, Patent still, Coffey still, sma' still, Highland still* and *Lowland still*.

**Stook** *v. and n.* (Scots) The traditional method of drying out harvested barley in the fields. This is done by stacking the sheaves of the harvested crop head to head in conical groups or *stooks*.

**Stot** (also **Stott, Stottin'**) *v.* (Scots) To stagger clumsily, while under the influence of alcohol. To rebound from walls.

**Stoup** *n.* (Scots) A deep narrow vessel for holding liquor, a measuring jug with a handle.

**Stoupfu'** *n.* (Scots) A full measure poured from a traditional stoup measuring jug.

**Stow** *n.* A row of casks, stored in a dunnage warehouse on layers. These rest on wooden duns or beams, up to a maximum of three rows high.

**Straikit-measure**

**Straikit-measure** *n.* (Scots) An exact measure of liquor.

**Strathclyde** – see **Grain distilleries**

**Strathspey** – see **Speyside**

**Streah** *n.* (Scots) A round of drinks. (From the Scots Gaelic **Sreath**) meaning a row or queue. Derives from the ancient tradition in the Western Isles of men gathering in a circle or parliament to discuss and decide on the issues and work priorities for the island. Each agreed decision was marked with a round or *sreath* of drink passed around in the **Cuach** or **Quaich**, a shared drinking vessel.

**Struite** *adj.* (Scots) Loud and vainglorious. Being filled with alcohol-induced bonhomie.

**Strule** *v.* (Scots) To pour from one liquor vessel into another.

**Stupid-fou** *adj.* (Scots) Stupidly drunk.

**Subtractive Maturation** *n.* During the maturation process the spirit undergoes three distinct changes. The first of these is subtractive maturation or removal. Straight from the pot still, new-make spirit has a clingy, metallic and rather unpleasant taste. Young whisky, bottled too soon after the required three years and a day have elapsed, is likely to still have this taste characteristic. Whisky at this age is not really worth bottling as a single malt, but the spirit may be used within a blend. The metallic taste dissipates as it matures in the cask and is usually gone after five to eight years. Few decent single malts are bottled until they have reached eight years.

**Suppable** *adj.* (Scots) Of liquor, agreeable for supping.

**Swag** (also **Sweg**) *n.* (Scots) A large measure of drink or liquor.

**Swalloch** (also **Sweel**) *n.* (Scots) A strong liquor. A rich foodstuff.

**Swan neck** *n.* The elongated copper neck at the top of the pot still that channels the distillate vapour from the still into the condenser. Swan necks can be tapered or straight-sided, long and narrow or short and abrupt. Usually the neck will have a porthole or two and even a light illuminating the interior, so that the still operator can observe any boiling occurring in the batch. The swan neck also usually has a **cold finger** at the top through which cold water is channelled. This serves to chill any hot foam which might otherwise find its way out of the still and into the condenser.

**Sweet associate** *n.* One of the key signature flavour elements identified in spirit distilled for whisky. Particularly apparent in whiskies which described as having hints of toffee, vanilla, custard powder and honey.

**Sweet-heap** *n.* (Scots) The mound of malted barley once it has been gathered up after being spread and dried on the malting barn floor.

**Swig** *v. and n.* To drink direct from the bottle next without pouring into a glass. A mouthful of liquor quickly taken.

**Swirl** *v. and n.* The most important action for visually appreciating a whisky after pouring into a glass. The spirit should be agitated around the sides of the glass. This is done by clutching the glass gently in the fist and rotating the glass in hand in a clockwise or anti-clockwise circular motion, thus oxygenating the spirit and releasing the aromas as well as revealing the heaviness, or oiliness, of the spirit by the legs of the spirit clinging to the glass.

**Switcher** *n.* The thin steel arm which rotates around the top of the washback, whipping through the head froth produced inside the vessel. As the wash liquor ferments, it produces huge amounts of foam and $CO_2$. While the gas is vented outside the wash room the frothing head is kept down, dealt with by the switcher inside the washback. Before automation this task was carried out manually by men who stood over the open washbacks beating the froth down with heather brooms.

**Synd** *n*. (Scots) A drink taken just after food to rinse or help digest.

**Sype** *v*. (Scots) To percolate or filter. To seep.

# T

**Tack** *n.* (Scots) The state of abstinence from alcohol for a period. Consciously avoiding and committing to going without alcohol for any period of time. Unlike going teetotal, asserting that one is *on the tack* implies that a return to drinking alcohol is planned, ironically perhaps when the benefits of abstinence i.e. increased health, wealth and social standing have been achieved.

**Tak** (also **Tak on**) *v.* (Scots) To drink out, or drain, a glass. To become tipsy, befuddled by drink.

**Taketsuru, Masataka** *n.* The Japanese man accorded the title the *'Father of Japanese Whisky'*. Masataka came to Glasgow to study organic chemistry at the University of Glasgow. In Japan his family had distilled and sold saké for generations. In Scotland he met and fell in love with Kirkintilloch girl Rita Cowan. In 1920 at a Glasgow Registry Office he secretly married his Scottish sweetheart, to the disapproval of both sets of parents. But it was Masataka's dream to bring *'real'*, traditional Scotch Whisky-making to Japan and the couple left that year for Japan to set about fulfilling it. He used the knowledge and experience he gained in Scotland, by his studies and a distillery apprenticeship, to meet the challenge of founding Japan's first whisky distillery. This was at Yamazaki, owned by the new Suntory company. Having achieved this first goal, Masataka left Suntory after three years to establish his own distillery in Yoichi, on Hokkaido. This location, bounded on three sides by mountains and on the fourth by the Sea of Japan, was chosen because of its similarities to Scotland's west coast landscape and weather. Masataka died in 1979 but his Nikka whisky company continues to produce some of the finest Japanese malt whisky and is a respected member of the global Scotch Whisky family.

**Talisker** *n.* Founded in 1830 by brothers Hugh and Kenneth Macaskill, Talisker was the only legal distillery on the Isle of Skye until 2017, when it acquired two new neighbours in Torabhaig in Sleat and the Isle of Raasay distillery. Its peaty malt was reputedly the favourite whisky of the writer Robert Louis Stevenson. The 20th century travel writer HV Morton also wrote eloquently of its inspirational *Sgitheanach* (Skye) character in his celebrated 1929 travelogue *In Search of Scotland*. *'As the Talisker burned in him it lit fires of patriotism, and I listened with delight as he spoke of his love for the hills and the glens and the peat-hags and the great winds and the grey mists.'*

**Tan** *v.* (Scots) To empty a bottle in a single session. To finish a drink with speed and enthusiasm, e.g. *We tanned the bottle by lunch time.*

**Tankard** (also **Tanker**) *n.* A simple cylindrical drinking vessel made from wood, clay or pewter, usually with a single handle. Tankard design took a quirky turn in the 19th century with the introduction of its strangely popular feature, a glass bottom. Its popularity, according to folk history, was because the glass bottom enabled the drinker, on draining the liquor in his raised tankard to see the room beyond. This alerted him to any possible approaching assailants or press gangs.

**Tand** *n.* (Scots) A piece of burning peat.

**Tanned** *adj.* (Scots) Of a drinking vessel, emptied.

**Tap** (also **Tap-tree**) *n.* (Scots) The wooden plug or bung used to seal the outlet or bunghole hole of a cask *v.* To borrow cash from a friend or acquaintance. To solicit funds on an informal short term basis for the buying the next round of drinks.

**Tarasgeir** (also **Turskil, Tushkar**) *n.* (Scots Gaelic) Traditional wooden long-handled, double-bladed, foot-driven tool for cutting and harvesting peat. Commonly used throughout the Western Isles and Highlands, the size and 90-degree angle of the two blades ensures the tarasgeir can slice through the wet peat to produce a uniformly-sized size slab of peat. The cut peat slabs are then stacked against each other on top of the peat bank for weeks of drying out. The cutters wait for a suitably windless day to arrive, usually at the height of the Hebridean summer. Then all available holidaymakers are invited out to the midgie-plagued moor beneath the baking sun for the unique, never to be forgotten experience of *'lifting the peats'*.

**Tasmania** *n.* In 2014 Tasmania's *Sullivan's Cove* was awarded the title of World's Best Single Malt Whisky, sparking global interest in Tasmanian whisky. This success and the recent burgeoning of the industry traces itself to a change in the law in the 1990s. This change overturned the government's historically proscriptive attitude towards whisky distilling dating back some 170 years. Back in 1838 Tasmania was very much like Scotland with its thriving whisky trade supplied by 16 legal distilleries operating throughout the island - and many more illegal ones. Whisky was widely available in both quantity and quality and in some echelons of society was deemed too readily available. At the time the Governor of Tasmania was John Franklin*. Commentators at the time characterised Franklin as a nice man but a rather indecisive and not very competent Governor. However, he did have a very persuasive and decisive advisor at his side in his wife, Lady Jane Franklin. She was a vehement opponent of alcohol and the spirit trade and regarded the ubiquity of whisky in her husband's territory as a personal affront. She famously proclaimed: *'I would prefer barley be fed to pigs than it be used to turn men into swine.'*

**Tass**

Such was her influence over Governor John that at her insistence he dutifully outlawed the distilling of spirits throughout Tasmania. In one fell swoop, the whisky industry was ruined. All distilleries were forced to close, never to reopen, and Tasmanian whisky ceased to exist. Somehow this situation was allowed to persist until the 1990s until one day land surveyor Bill Lark stopped for an outdoor dram while fishing in the Tasmanian Highlands. Then Bill, surrounded by pure, clear mountain water, rich fields of barley and peat in abundance, had his *'uisge beatha!'* moment. He realised he was smack bang in the middle of perfect whisky making country. His research uncovered the reason why, despite its natural suitability, Tasmania produced no whisky. He successfully campaigned for Lady Franklin's archaic law to be overturned and Tasmania rejoined the free whisky world. Bill and his wife Lyn set about founding the Lark Distillery, the first legal distillery in Tasmania for 150 years. With its natural **terroir** attributes a mirror image of Scotland, the island of Tasmania is now recognised as one of the world's key whisky players with nine distilleries spread across the island. Tasmania is once again producing whisky on a par with Scotland' with a secure, long term future as a mature whisky region.

* After his posting as Governor of Tasmania Sir John Franklin went on to write his own tragic chapter in history with the disastrous Franklin Arctic expedition which led to the loss of HMS *Terror* and all 129 lives in the party.

**Tass** *n.* (Scots) A goblet or drinking cup, often ornate and crafted from pewter or silver, made principally for spirits. A drinking vessel or bowl. Features in Scots poet Allan Ramsay's 1725 poem 'The Gentle Shepherd'; *'Fill him up a tass of usqaebae...'* Also **Tassie**. Robert Burns' 1788 poem has the line, *'Go, fetch to me a pint o' wine, and fill it in a silver tassie.'*

**Taste** *v.* To drink alcohol in small amounts for the purpose of sample comparison or expressing opinion. To sip or tipple. The sensory identification of flavour elements in a whisky occurring through *gustation*. This happens when the spirit is brought into contact with the 5000 or so taste buds located in and around the oral cavity as it is rolled around the mouth.

**Tastin'** *n.* (Scots) An impromptu drinking session on the chance meeting of friends. A drinking of drams in company. Time set aside for enjoyment of whisky and friendship.

**Tasting** *n.* A formal social event where whisky enthusiasts come together with industry professionals, producers and commentators to critically examine and enjoy a selection of different whiskies. A typical tasting will focus on three to six whiskies, ranging across a spectrum of age, cask type, non-peated to heavily peated. The selected whiskies are poured into dramming glasses and placed around the communal table. Each participant is issued with their own tasting booklet to capture their own flavour notes and opinions. The host begins the tasting, introducing each whisky in sequence. Peated whiskies are normally left to the end due to their pungency. Each whisky is sampled, first by sight, then by nose, then by taste. The host invites comment and opinion around the table until all have been sampled and the most popular agreed upon. Full agreement might require further samplings/tastings.

**Teem** *v.* (Scots) To pour generously into a glass or drinking vessel. To fill to overflowing.

**Tee-tee** *n.* (Scots) A teetotaller. Someone who abstains from drinking alcohol.

**Temperance** *n.* Despite intense lobbying against it by the brewers and distillers, the Temperance Scotland Act was successfully passed in 1913 in response to the campaigning of the countrywide

Temperance Movement. Their aim was to prohibit the sale of alcohol in areas of Scotland's towns and cities wherever the local population demanded it. The Act specified the strict conditions required to prohibit the sale of alcohol in an area based on the outcome of a local referendum. There were three options presented for the vote: no change, a 25% reduction in licenses to sell alcohol, or complete abolition of all existing licences. The final option required at least 55% support from voters, and at least 35% of everyone registered to vote in the constituency. If this threshold was not achieved then the votes cast in support counted towards the 25% reduction option.

This led to the establishment and proliferation of a patchwork of urban 'dry' areas. These were particularly numerous in cities such as Glasgow where 'respectable' districts voted to outlaw pubs. But the prohibition was also limited. There was no proscription of the manufacture of alcoholic beverages, nor of their wholesaling, or their consumption in private. These dry areas were also often undermined by local authorities permitting licenses to selected hotels and restaurants. These were allowed on the proviso that alcohol was only served to customers having 'a meal'. This meal requirement was open to wide interpretation and was often 'met' by serving the customer with an opened pack of crisps. The Act was superseded by the *Licensing (Scotland) Act 1959* until these provisions and the local polls were abolished by the *Licensing (Scotland) Act 1976*.

**Terroir** *n.* (French) Combined environmental, climatic and landscape influences on a natural food or beverage product cultivated or produced there. Originating in French wine husbandry, the term defines the unique characteristics attributed to the location where a foodstuff is produced. In Scotch whisky production *terroir* roughly corresponds to the protected regions of each whisky type. However, simple definitions of Highland, Lowland, Speyside, Islay and Campbeltown don't fully convey the diversity of the key influences influencing whisky production. Nor do they reflect the character of spirit distilled in the specific locale of each individual distillery. Whisky terroir influences include; origin of the barley, air source and humidity, air quality in malting, geological origins and quality of the water source, coastal exposure to salt sea air, altitude, and ongoing climactic influences such as average local air temperature ranges. All of these factors combine to convey many distinct distillery characteristics which influence the whisky's aroma, taste and finish.

**Teuchter** *n.* (Scots) A colourful, if slightly disparaging, term used to describe a Highlander, Gaelic speaker or indeed anyone with any authentic rural, non-metropolitan Scottish accent. The word implies someone who is unschooled in the high culture and sophisticated ways of the city and the culture of the savvy, wine bar-dwelling, Subway-riding *Weegie*.

**Tew** *v.* Of grain, to become moist. To dampen so that the batch of grain spoils and takes on a musty taint.

    *n.* (Scots) An unpleasant, musty taste caused by dampness in the grain batch. Despite the intensity of the distillation temperatures and length of the process, the tew may survive into the new-make spirit. It may also survive throughout the maturation in the cask and noticeably taint the finished whisky flavour when poured into the glass

**Thief** *n.* (Scots) Also known as the **Dog** due to its attached 'lead'. This test tube-shaped brass vessel is a key accessory to the distillery worker's personal 'equipment' as he or she goes about the casks stored in the warehouses. Crafted to the exact measurements of the bung hole, it is weighted for dipping into the cask. The thief sinks down into the heart of the cask, fills with a good measure of the spirit and is lifted for sampling. A handy and essential tool for each distillery worker that does exactly what the name says. Especially useful for those with an interest in monitoring the quality and taste of the whisky as it evolves during the maturation process. Handily, the slim nature of its design also enables it to be carried unseen in the fold of a jacket or well-tailored trouser leg.

**Thirds** *n.* (Scots) Brewers' grains.

**Thrapple** *n.* (Scots) The throat or gullet as in; *'A wee dram tae douse the thrapple, sir?'*

**Tiff** *v. and n.* (Scots) To down liquor, to quaff. A small draught or drink.

**Till** *n.* (Scots) Liquor in general. Drink. Stuff.

**Tim** *v.* (Scots) To pour out a vessel. To empty.

**Tinkle-sweetie** *n.* (Scots) The traditional eight o'clock evening bell which rang out in Edinburgh. This signalled time for shops and trades to close for the night. Folk should now make their way to their howffs and taverns to discuss the day's business and affairs.

**Tip** (also **Tipney, Tippenize**) *v.* To drink off. To down. To tipple small beer.
    *n.* (Scots) Ale sold for two pence a pint.

**Tippeny-hoose** *n.* (Scots) A cheap ale or liquor house.

**Tipsie** *n.* (Scots) Any alcoholic drink or liquor.

**Toast** *v.* In company, to offer a celebratory salutation in praise or fond expression of a person, persons, place or event. The marking of the moment with a call and response to the assembled company invoking the subject of the toast, e.g. *'The Bride* *and Groom!'* This is repeated by the crowd followed by the concerted downing of a measure from a charged glass of good whisky (or some other suitably hearty beverage). Also, to tease publicly.

    *n.* A celebratory invocation to a company, inviting all to drink in mark of agreement to the expressed sentiment.

**Toasting** *n.* Not the traditional raising of the glass but a key process in cask production and triggering maturation. Once a new cask has been assembled from the staves, reeds and metal hoops it is ready to be activated as a living breathing womb. It must now be made ready to receive and interact with spirit in the maturation. To achieve this the oak cask is *'toasted'* for around 30 minutes inside a large oven at 200°C. This sustained heat degrades the wood's polymers by fracturing the rigid cellulose structures to release flavour compounds in the wood. The toasting also ensures any raw, resinous residues or unpleasant aroma compounds in the wood which might influence flavour are destroyed. Toasting also causes caramelisation of the wood sugars and plays a key role in releasing desirable flavour and colour compounds. It produces aromatic **aldehydes** and acids which oxydise as the spirit penetrates the wood. Characteristically this converts **lignin** in the wood into important aromatic compounds for the maturing whisky such as **vanillin** and vanillic acid. Once it has been thoroughly toasted, a cask is made ready to receive the new-make spirit and so begin the process of maturation.

**Tòiseach** *n.* (Scots Gaelic) The traditional *chieftain* or *thane* of a Highland or island area. The hereditary representative of the crown and local leader who administered justice, gave out licences and permits and collected rents. Ferintosh Distillery takes its name from *Fearann Toisich* 'the lands of the Toiseach' around the Black Isle. The term is still used for the Irish Prime Minister (but spelt *Taoiseach*).

# Toddy

**Toddy** *n.* (From the Scots Gaelic ***Todaidh***) The centuries-old, traditional, self-medicating home-made liquor treatment for cold or flu symptoms. *'Hot toddies'* are usually recommended and created by a sympathetic friend for someone who is unquestionably 'miserable with the cold'. The combination of whisky, hot water, sugar and honey creates a potent liquor which courses through the blood delivering legendary curative properties. Key symptoms targeted by the toddy are runny nose, sore throat, and sniffling. The alcohol in the whisky dilates the blood vessels, acting as a decongestant and helping mucus membranes deal with the infection. Similarly, the hot diluted sugars and inhaling the liquorous steam helps clear the body's cold symptoms. Finally, the key recommendation is timing. Toddies should be taken just before bed to ensure their effectiveness and feel-good benefits are concentrated at the optimum time when the body is ready for rest and recovery. However, it must be remembered that while one generous hot toddy is good medicine, two generous toddies may cause new symptoms. Such as hiccups and singing.

**Toom** *v.* (Scots) To empty. To neck or drink a vessel to finish.

**Toom-the stoup** *n.* (Scots) A drouth, habitual drinker, a drunken fellow.

**Toot** *v. and n.* (Scots) To drink copiously. To tipple. A copious draught of liquor. A drinking bout.

**Toothfu'** *v.* (Scots) To tipple. To drink in small quantities.
*n.* A small sensation of whisky. A moderate tasting. A tincture.

**Tootie** (also **Tooty**) *n.* (Scots) A dram. A drunkard.

**Tootle** (also **Tootlin**) *v.* (Scots) Tippling straight from the bottle at regular but short intervals.

**Tootlie** *adj* (Scots) Unsteady in walking from drink. Staggeringly drunk.

**Tosg** *n.* (Scots Gaelic) A peat-cutting tool.

**Tosie** *n.* (Scots) A cheery glow on the cheeks. A rosiness on the face while drinking alcohol.
    *adj.* Slightly intoxicated. Merry. Happy. Tipsy.

**Toss** *v.* To toast. To drink to the health of. A toast.
    *n.* (Scots) A beauty who is often the popular subject of toasts.

**Tossie** *adj.* (Scots) Unsteady from intoxication. Tipsy.

**Toss-pot** *n.* (Scots) A habitual drinker. A well-known drunken fellow. A drouth.

**Tot** *n.* (Scots) A wee dram. A shot. A splash.

**Totaller** *n.* (Scots) Someone who abstains from drinking alcohol. A teetotaller.

**Tout** (also **Touter**) *v. and n.* (Scots) To drink copiously. A large measure. A generous pour.

**Treacle-ale** (also **Treacle-beer, Treacle-peerie**) *n.* (Scots) A thin light beer made with treacle.

**Treetle** *v. and n.* (Scots) To trickle small drops. A small drop.

**Trestarig** *n.* (Scots) From the Gaelic *Treas-tarruing* meaning *three distillations*. A very strong spirit encountered and described in 1703 by the traveller Martin Martin in his travels around the Hebrides:

'Their plenty of corn was such, as disposed the natives to brew several sorts of liquor, as common Usquebaugh, another called Trestarig, i.e. Aquavitae, three times distill'd, which is strong and hot'.

**Tryphtophan** *n.* In fermentation of the wort, tryptophan is one of the group of slowly absorbed amino acids. The others are **phenylalanine**, **alanine**, **glycine** and **tyrosine** which are synthesised and absorbed by the yeast as it goes into next generation bud stage.

**Tub** *n.* (Scots) A smuggler's small, easily transportable keg containing four gallons.

**Tun** *n.* Large cylindrical brewing vessel in which the first stage of the *'cooking'* process of the malted barley occurs. Originally tuns were open cast-iron vessels heated directly underneath by coal or peat. The liquor inside was rotated by hand using long-handled wooden paddles. These have been replaced with the enclosed and mechanised **Lauter** tun. These mild steel mashing vessels deliver continuous temperature-controlled sparge water, efficient rotation and flow management. The rotating lauter blades in the mash tun can be raised, lowered and planed to ensure maximum sugar extraction from the grist into the wort liquid. At the end of the mashing the wort liquid is extracted via the perforated mashtun floor and fed through to the washbacks for fermentation.

**Tup-horn** *n.* (Scots) A ram's horn fashioned into a drinking vessel.

**Turning-tree** *n.* (Scots) A long-handled wooden stirring tool for mashing. A spurtle.

**Turskil** (also **Tushkar**) *n.* (Scots) A spade for cutting peat. The traditional long-handled, double-bladed, foot-driven wooden-shafted tool for harvesting peat. The size and angle of the two blades ensures that the cutter can slice through the wet peat and produce a uniformly sized size slab of peat. These are placed in small stacks on top of the peat bank for weeks of drying by the Atlantic winds before collection later in the summer.

**Turven** *n*. (Scots) Cut turfs of peat. Sods.

**Tusk** (also **Tushk**) *v*. (Scots) To cut peat from above, using the Tushkar or Tarasgeir.

**Tutie** *n*. (Scots) A flirtatious female tippler.

**Tyrosine** *n*. In fermentation of the wort, a slowly absorbed amino acid belonging to the group including alanine, glycine, phenylalanine and tryptophan.

# u

**Uisge Beatha** *n.* (Scots Gaelic, 'Water of Life'). The etymological root of 'whisky' is a combination of the two Scots Gaelic words, *Uisge* (Pron; oosh'kuh) meaning *'water'* in English and *Beatha* (Pron; beh'hah) meaning *'life'*. The evolution of the Gaelic name for the Latin *Aqua Vitae* towards the generic word whisky derives from the growth in popularity of Highland whisky from the 1730s. Scots Gaelic was the dominant language throughout the Scottish Highland hinterland at that time and the producers and makers and traders of uisge beatha conducted their business in that language. The popularity of Highland whisky in Scotland meant that the Gaelic name became a differentiating mark of the 'good stuff', setting it apart from the sharper, hot spirit being produced in the Lowlands. The popularity of Highland uisge beatha grew throughout the British Isles in the 18th and 19th centuries as the Napoleonic Wars and **Phylloxera** brandy crash increased demand for good Scotch whisky. This dragged the Gaelic name across into Scots then English, filtered through the linguistic tics and accents of these languages. Uisge beatha evolved to become ushka then whiska before being formally written in documents in the 19th century as whisky whilst Irish spirit was being defined in written form as whiskey. However, this phonetic confection, and linguistically mongrel word 'whisky' unfortunately lost its meaningful and descriptive original components of *water* and *life*. But then part of the pleasure of being a Scotch whisky lover is peeling off the label and discovering the history, the complexities, the origins and tradition behind the seeming simplicity of the spirit in the glass.

## Uisge-beatha-braiche

**Uisge-beatha-braiche** *n.* (Scots Gaelic) Malt whisky. Literally *malted water of life*.

**Umbrella Aroma** *n.* The broad initial categories used when assessing the characteristics of a whisky poured into a tasting glass. These are **floral, fruity, cereal, woody, winey, feint** and **sulphur**. Called 'umbrella aromas' because they give the overarching character of the whisky under which more subtle, subjective and distinctive sub-aromas and flavour notes can be detected and described. These seven represent a starting point for whisky enthusiasts nosing a whisky for the first time. They act as a first step or key to accessing and identifying the secondary flavours and aromas. In tastings, they are represented in the form of a Scotch whisky '**flavour spectrum**' or '**flavour wheel**' which is a handy visual way of identifying and capturing the category of whisky aroma and taste.

**Underback** *n.* The balancing tank beside the mashtun. Used by the mashman as an aid to ensure the wort is not drawn off too quickly. In the mashing process the underback acts as an intermediate vessel before the wort reaches the washbacks. Its purpose is to act as a reservoir or buffer to ensure the grist is not drawn down onto the false bottom of the mash tun, blocking the drainage slots.

**Under bond** *adj.* The classification of any quantity of whisky sold on which the Excise Duty has not yet been paid. This whisky may be consigned for storage in a bonded warehouse for an undefined period but cannot be released for retail sale until such times as the duty is paid and it can be reclassified and marked as *Duty Paid*.

**Undercooking** *n.* In the mashing of the malt grist, undercooking can occur if the water temperature is not hot enough or the mashing period is too brief. This significantly reduces the amount of alcohol yield of a batch since hydrolysis is curtailed. This affects the amount of starch that can easily be accessed by the enzyme actions and the

222

fermentable sugars for alcohol production. At the other end of the scale, overcooking can similarly lock out the enzymes and reduce yield by causing sticking, clumping and caramelising of the mash.

**Undermoor** *n.* In peat cutting, the cutters work together on two levels. The first cutter takes the topmost cut or *Uppermoor* and the other, following on, takes the next cut from the newly exposed lower level or Undermoor.

**Unforlattit** *adj.* (Scots) Of wine or liquor, new-make. Fresh.

**Uppermoor** *n.* The topmost level of the cut peat bank above the lower Undermoor.

**Uptake** *n.* The rate of water uptake in a barley grain. In malting barley, uptake is a key factor in the final spirit yield derived from any batch of malt. The barley must be tricked into believing 'spring has sprung' to access the sugars stored in the grain. This involves a three stage 'steeping' of the barley batch in water lasting around 50 hours with controlled temperature change. The process progresses with alternate drying and consistent agitation of the grains to ensure thorough and even moisture and temperature conditions. In modern distilling, careful laboratory measurements are made of grain samples from each batch. Water uptake tests on these grains determine firstly that the exposure to water will trigger water uptake and that the batch is not completely dormant. The test also measures the rate at which the grains will absorb water at certain temperatures to predict the likely uptake performance of a batch.

These measurements are necessary to guide decisions on the length of time and temperature for the crucial first steeping of the batch. In the first steep, enzyme activity is triggered at around 25% saturation. When it reaches around 35% the soaking batch is drained and ventilated. This second phase is the lag or air-rest. This lasts another ten hours, allowing the moist grain membranes to soften and the germination process and enzyme activity inside the grain to progress. Chitting, or germination, occurs at this point as the roots and shoots start to emerge from the germ of the grain. The third stage of the steeping soaks the batch again to maximise the water uptake and ensure the grain is fully hydrated and the embryo reaches optimum 85% saturation to drive the chitting and the production of sugars in the grain.

**Urquhart family** – see **Gordon and MacPhail**

**Usher** *n.* Andrew Usher II (1782-1855) is the distiller recognised as the creator of the first commercially successful blended Scotch whisky brand and is one of the key figures in the history of Scotch whisky's evolution as a global phenomenon. His blend's O.V.G. brand initials stood for *'Old Vatted Glenlivet'*. In the 1850s, Usher bought up all the output from the Glenlivet distillery on Speyside and created a vatted malt, then a recipe for a blend. Usher is credited with ensuring a consistent and repeatable blend for vatting and bottling a blended whisky for the first time. He was one of the three founders of the North British distillery in Edinburgh which remains today the world's second largest producer of Scotch whisky. He is also celebrated as the benefactor who donated £100,000 to the City of Edinburgh for the building of the world-famous Usher Concert Hall.

**Usque** *n.* (Scots) One of the many Scots spelling variations of the Gaelic name uisge beatha meaning 'water of life'. Other recorded regional variations include *usqeba, usquebae, usquebagh, usquabae, usquebey* and *usquibue*.

**Usquebaugh** *n.* (Gaeilge) Traditionally the phonetic English spelling for any generic Irish distilled spirit including *poiteen*.

# V

**Valine** *n.* In fermentation of the wort, valine is one of the slower group of amino acids absorbed at the beginning of the fermentation process. This grouping includes **isoleucine, leucine, methionine** and **histidine**. These are among the first to be synthesised as the yeast feeds and expands on the sugar in the wort.

**Vanillin** *n.* One of the earliest and most distinctive flavour elements arising from the oak wood and active in maturation, vanillin is one of the most identifiable aldehydes as wood and spirit interact. A significant element in the oak wood's **lignin**, vanillin is one of the **aldehydes** which reaches its flavour threshold early in the maturation period. Charring the inner surface of the cask by direct flame or baking the wood's surface breaks open the surface membrane to ensure vanillin can be accessed by the spirit when the cask is filled. As the spirit penetrates the wood so the vanillin is released to be absorbed by the spirit and add flavour throughout its time in the cask.

**Vapour** *n.* The magical intermediate form of the spirit in the still as the heated alcohol in the wash and low wines vapourises and **ethanol** takes to the air. As it rises the vapour is recirculated through the maelstrom of the reflux chamber. It rides the hot current up through the still head, through the lye arm and down into the cooling condensers. Now the vapourised alcohol reforms as a liquid. Vapour also occurs in the less dynamic but heady form of the spirit that hangs in the air inside the bonded warehouses.

**Vat**

This is the **Angels' Share**, the whisky that evaporates through the wood of the casks at a rate of roughly 1% per annum in Scotland.

**Vat** *v.* To mix different whiskies together in a large vessel for a period of time to achieve a particular flavour. Pioneered by Andrew Usher in the mid-19th century. He created a brand in its own right as the *Old Vatted Glenlivet* or *O.V.G.* by mixing different batches and distillations of Glenlivet in a vat for bottling as a unique blended product.

    *n.* A large capacity vessel such as tub or tank for mixing or storing liquids.

**Vat 69** *n.* Perhaps the most perfunctory but effective and enduring brand name of all. In 1882 William Sanderson filled 100 vats with different mixes of specially chosen whiskies which he let *marry* for a time. When they had lain long enough he tasked some expert noses from the industry with sampling each of the hundred vats and giving their verdicts. The overwhelming response was that Vat no 69 was the superior blend. So the brand was born and its name decided in the simplest manner. Currently owned by Diageo, Vat 69 remains one of the world's top selling whiskies, shipping over 1.5 million nine-litre cases each year across the globe.

**Victual** *n.* (Scots) Any corn or grain, before or after harvesting.

**Victualler** *n.* (Scots) A dealer or merchant who deals in grains, meal and cereals.

**Viking whisky** *adj.* The growth in Scandinavian whisky production, particularly in the single malt, specialist finish, sector has brought the recent concept of *Viking whisky* to the market. Many Scottish distilleries, especially on Orkney, the islands and west coast have also produced malts named in honour of the Norse culture that left its mark in place names such as Talisker, the distillery on Skye

**Villa Nova, Arnold de** *n.* The 13th century physician and apothecary who was first to record the distillation of wine and the beneficial results of drinking it.

**Vintage** *n.* The defined year of bottling a distillation of whisky. This must clearly be displayed on labels and packaging. Scotch Whisky Regulations require that only one year may be identified on the packaging and that all of the whisky in the product must have been distilled in that year. At bottling, the whisky must be packaged with clear information stating either the year of bottling or an age statement. All bottles must feature labels or packaging stating the year of bottling or the age statement and the year of distillation or vintage.

**Vintner** *n.* A merchant who deals in wines and spirits. A merchant who buys, sells, supplies and sometimes produces wines and liquors.

**Virgin Oak** *n.* One of the most popular cask finishings for some expressions of single malt. Virgin oak casks are chosen for the vanilla and almond flavour elements contained within the new oak. Most whisky is matured in used bourbon casks which have already given out these flavour elements into the bourbon. Whisky matured in virgin oak therefore brings a fresh palette of colour, aroma and flavour that distinguishes it from those matured in used bourbon, sherry, port or wine casks.

**Virl** (also **Virrel**) *n.* (Scots) The iron band, or ring, fixed tightly round a cask to seal the staves together and ensure the cask does not leak. A ringed ferrule.

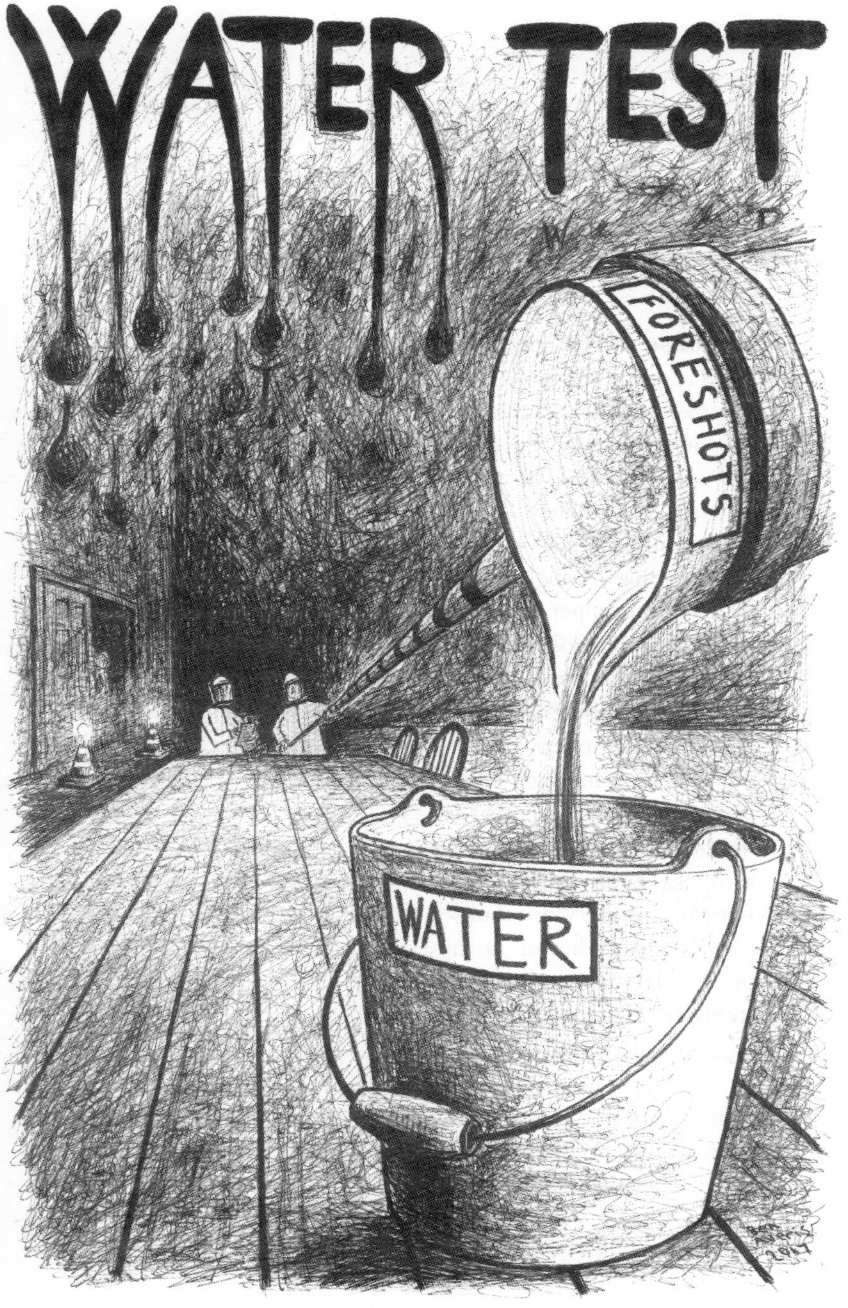
WATER TEST
FORESHOTS
WATER

# W

**Warehouse** *n.* The dark, silent citadel of any distillery where the filled casks lie for three years and a day in racks, faintly breathing out the **Angels' Share** as the spirit matures within and slowly evaporates through the oak membrane. Warehouses are designed to maintain cool, dark and dry conditions allowing natural interaction between ambient air and the ethanol-heavy air inside the cask. Historically, distillery warehouses are traditional stone, timber and slate buildings of single or multiple storeys with cinder ground floor and wooden upper floors, located on the distillery site. Storage methods inside will vary, depending on age and capacity. Older, traditional 'dunnage' warehouses use simple wooden duns or beams to *stow* casks in layers on top of each other, supported simply by the duns. Modern rack warehouses have much greater vertical capacity by using high steel frame racks accessed using elevator platforms. More recently, palletised warehousing has become the most efficient method of mechanised cask handling with usually six casks stored upright on pallets stored up to six pallets high. On site, distillery warehouses vary in size and number and are a rough visual indicator of the capacity and annual production of the distillery. Warehouses are also important in distinguishing the **'terroir'** identity of single malt brands whose whisky spends its entire formative life in the distillery catchment before being sent for bottling. These contrast with brands whose casks are removed from their home environment to be transported and finished with casks from multiple distilleries in vast bonded warehouses in the Central Belt and elsewhere.

**Warehouse staining** *n*. The matt black colouration often found on the exterior walls of bonded warehouses which house casks of maturing whisky. This staining is caused by a fungus *Baudoinia compniacensis* which flourishes on timber and woodland, at distillery locations. Popularly known as the **Angels' Share Fungus** it thrives on the **ethanol** vapour which evaporates through the filled oak casks. Over time, the matt black layer of the fungus infiltrates and overtakes the timber's natural grain and colour. *Baudoinia compniacensis fungus* was first identified in brandy warehouses in the Cognac region of France. With twenty million casks of whisky lying maturing at any one time the fungus naturally also thrives in Scotland, even in the coldest and bleakest distillery locations. Indeed, arrays of brooding, blackened warehouses standing out against a bare moorland are a characteristic motif of the Scottish whisky landscape.

**Wash** *n*. A beery alcoholic liquor produced after the fermentation cycle of the wort has been completed in the washbacks. The sugar-rich liquor pumped through from the mashtun is transformed by fermenting distiller's yeast within 48 hours into a pale beer or ale of between 7-11% ABV. All the sugars present in the wort liquor are converted into alcohol and the by-product $CO_2$ vapour which is vented outside.

**Wash Act** *n*. Introduced in 1784 following the end of the American War of Independence and the Highland famine of 1783 the Wash Act was crafted to reduce the use of barley for illicit distilling, reduce the revenue burden on distillers and simplify collection of duty. This new duty was based on projected production capacity. It charged a rate of 5d (five pence) for every gallon of wash, as opposed to the more complex tax calculation hitherto based on the quantity of distilled low wines and spirit. It was reckoned that every five gallons of wash would produce one gallon of spirit so that each gallon of spirit raised 2 shillings 1d in tax. The Wash Act also removed the historic exemption from duty enjoyed by the **Ferintosh** distillery which had enabled the Forbes of Culloden family to gain a unique subsidised advantage over all other highland whisky producers. After a century of such advantage the removal of the exemption caused the distillery to close within a year, causing no less a poet than Robert Burns to pine, *'Thee Ferintosh, O sadly lost...'*

**Washback** *n.* The large cylindrical vat, tub or vessel at the heart of a distillery where the fermentation of the sugar-rich wort takes place. Washbacks are the low-tech, unsung workhorses of any distillery, made from wood or stainless steel. Wooden washbacks are generally made from Oregon pine/Douglas fir, or larch. In the wash room the sugary wort liquor arrives from the mashtuns, filling into these deep, dark wells. Then yeast is added and natural fermentation kicks off. Within 48 hours the sugary wort is transformed into an alcoholic wash, a citrusy, beery liquor of between 7-11% ABV.

**Wash Charger** *n.* Once fully fermented in the washback, the transformed liquor now has an alcoholic by volume (ABV) content of around 7-11% ABV. The next stage before distillation is running the wash liquor through to fill the wash charger. This is a large tank or reservoir, usually located overhead in the still house. The wash charger has the capacity to hold a full batch of wash liquor, ready for running into the wash still. This first distillation transforms the wash into **Low Wines**, a more intense alcoholic liquor of around 25% ABV.

**Wash Still** *n.* The wash still is the first and largest of the copper pot stills in the still house. It functions like a kettle. Direct or indirect heat is applied to the still, gently boiling the wash liquor until it causes the alcohol to evaporate and travel up the still neck. Inside the still, flavouring compounds or **congeners** form as the heated and volatile vapour interacts with the copper surface.

Temperature is reduced to keep the wash simmering below the boil, to avoid solids attaching to the copper surface and spoiling the distillation. Most wash stills have sight glasses on their neck to allow the still operator to observe the volatility inside the still. The complex ethanol vapour passes out from the still across the angled **Lye arm** and down into the **condenser**. The operator usually has the option of using the **cold finger** device to halt any rising froth that might mix with the condensing vapour. In the condenser, the vapour meets cold air, causing it to return to a liquid form. Now the liquor has 'reformed' as Low Wines with an ABV rating of about 25% ABV. ˙

**Watchman** *n*. The worker tasked with responsibility for monitoring a bonded warehouse's ambient conditions, its structural maintenance and the condition and security of the casks stored within. Leakage from casks happens. Each year a distillery will expect to find at least one cask which has lost its precious contents. However, a more positive task in the watchman's role is the tasting and collection of samples from casks for the Malt Master or Master Blender to consider for bottling or blending.

**Water** *n*. In a country as wet as Scotland, it is a happy coincidence that the most important, fundamental ingredient in the production of Uisge Beatha, the water of life, whisky, is of course, *uisge* or water. Otherwise known as H2O, water is necessary to every stage of the whisky-making process. The secret of Scotch whisky's special quality is often ascribed to 'something in the water'. All distillers are very precious about their source. Many claim all sorts of unique terroir influences that can be traced through from the burn to the final finish of the whisky in the cask. These can range from infinitesimally small geological traces to visible particles of peat floating in the distillery pond. The fact is that without water there would be no whisky. It is the very medium that conveys all other ingredients and

elements, from the first steeping of the barley to the filling of
the bottle. Indeed, to the mouth of the final consumer. Good
water supply and management is therefore vital in terms of spirit
quality, volume and temperature. Without it there would be no
successful malting, mashing, fermentation, distilling, cask filling
and finally, bottling. It also significantly helps with the pouring,
tasting and swallowing. Thankfully Scotland is also home to the
legendary water spirits, the mysterious Kelpies that inhabit and
guard all our watercourses.

**Water test** *n*. A test carried out during the spirit run in the still house
to identify the quality of the liquor running through the still as
being 'middle cut' or 'heart'. The still operator mixes foreshots
with water to decide when to select the heart of the spirit for the
batch. This is an observational test conducted in the spirit safe. At
first the mixture will appear milky and turbid. When the samples
show clear then the spirit is judged to be in potable condition. The
still operator will change the direction of the spirit flow pipe and
send the run for collection in the spirit receiver.

**Water Tub** *n*. A simple vat or vessel used for condensing in small-
scale still systems. The worm leading from the pot still is immersed
into its cold water, cooling and condensing the distilled ethanol
vapour to liquid form.

**Weem** *n*. (Scots, from Gaelic **uamh**) A natural cave by a sea shore.
Traditionally used by whisky smugglers for storage and distribution.

**Wee-skee** *excl*. In Latin America photographers ask their subjects to
say *'Wee-skee!'* so that they smile in the same way as *'Cheese!'* is used
in English speaking countries.

**Wet** *v. and adj*. (Scots) To proffer or take a small quantity of drink

**Whack**

purely as a social gesture, e.g. *'I'll hae a wee wet of the thrapple'*. Given to drink.

**Whack** *v.* To drink rapidly and copiously with attendant gulping noises. *n.* (Scots) A large measure of drink.

**Whawkie** *n.* (Scots) Whisky.

**Wheep** *n.* (Scots) Whisky at a penny a bottle.

**Wheich** *n.* (Scots) Whisky.

**Whigmaleerie** *n.* (Scots) An old drinking club game, played using pins. Nowadays a whim or trifle.

**Whisk** *n.* (Scots) A whisky.

**Whiskied** *adj.* (Scots) Drunk with whisky, tipsy.

**Whisky** *n.* The name arose in the 18th century as the common usage for the spirit distilled in the Highlands. It may be that the *'wh'* of whisky came about due to a long night of Dr Samuel Johnson asking a Highlander to repeatedly say the words *'Uisge Beatha'*. In his 1755 Dictionary, Dr Johnson recorded from personal encounter his account of the very word that has come to be the modern defined spelling for Scotch *'Whisky'*. He records, *'The highland sort is someone hotter and by corruption, in Scottish "they"* [presumably meaning the Lowland Scots] *"call it whisky".'* A hundred years later T. Thomson was recording in *Notes on Scottish Brewing* that: *'The whisky made by smugglers in Scotland is universally preferred by the inhabitants, and is purchased at a higher price, under the name of Highland whisky. This is partly owing to its being made entirely from malt.'*

**Whiskybae** *n.* (Scots) Usquebaugh. Whisky.

**Whisky-bukky** *n.* (Scots) A traditional mixture of oatmeal and whisky rolled together to form a ball of meal.

**Whisky-can** *n.* (Scots) Any suitable drinking vessel from which whisky can be drunk.

**Whisky-fair** *n.* (Scots) Any drunken revel. A gathering for drinking whisky.

**Whisky Galore** *n.* The 1947 book by Compton Mackenzie which inspired the 1949 Sandy MacKendrick-directed Ealing studio film of the same name. Both told the story of the freighter *SS Politician* which foundered on rocks off the small Hebridean island of Eriskay in 1941. Despite the wartime peril of the seas around the British Isles, the 8,000-tonne cargo ship set sail from Liverpool bound for Kingston, Jamaica with 28,000 cases of malt whisky. Against the background of wartime sacrifice and austerity the arrival on the shores of the Hebrides of such a bounty was quickly recognised by islanders as an historic salvage opportunity. In a race against time, tide and an expedition of Customs and Excise officers the skilled local seamen set about 'rescuing' the whisky and bringing it ashore. Their efforts succeeded in salvaging thousands of cases which were stored and distributed throughout the islands before the government **Excise Officers** or Gaugers could access and monitor the wreck. In 2013 two bottles of whisky salvaged in 1987 by local Donald MacPhee, sold for £12,050 after an online auction. In 2016 Scots director Gillies Mackinnon released a remake of the classic Ealing film.

**Whisky house** *n.* (Scots) A public house serving whisky but with no bar.

**Whisky-maker** *n.* (Scots) A distiller.

**Whisky-pig** *n*. (Scots) A ceramic jar for storing and carrying whisky.

**Whisky-pistol** *n*. (Scots) An easily concealed whisky hip flask.

**Whisky-plash** *n*. (Scots) A plentiful supply of the spirit in a drinking bout.

**Whisky-spore** *n*. (Scots) A drunken revel.

**Whisky-tacket** *n*. (Scots) An obvious, inflamed facial pimple caused by over indulgence in strong liquor.

**Whisky-wife** *n*. (Scots) A woman who sells whisky.

**White Lightning** *n*. Otherwise known as *Moonshine, Hooch, Mountain Dew, White Whiskey, White Liquor, Homebrew, Corn liquor* etc. High-proof spirits distilled in certain parts of the United States using a corn mash as the main ingredient. Especially associated with the Appalachian Mountains.

**Willie Arnot** *n*. (Scots) Traditional slang name for any good whisky as in, *'Sure that dram's the very Willie Arnot!'*

**Wine** *n*. The first accounts of the distillation of wine date to the early 13th century. These are distinct from much earlier and more ancient alembic perfumery distillations of roses and other flowers. The impact of these first distillations of wine are evidenced by the reactions of such as the physician Arnold de Villa Nova. He learned the Arabian technique of distilling ethyl alcohol from wine and excitedly wrote of the *'discovery of a panacea that humanity had been waiting for!'*

**Wishy washy** *adj*. (Scots) Any weak or watery drink or liquor.

**Wizzen** *n.* (Scots) The gullet or throat.

**Wobbling-shop** *n.* (Scots) An unlicensed whisky drinking shop.

**Wood** *n.* Oak and Oregon pine are the two key wood elements in the production of whisky. Oak, whether American or European, is the wood used for crafting the casks in which the whisky will lie. Here it matures, absorbing the wood's colour and flavour for a minimum of three years. As the spirit matures in the cask the oak wood's influence on the whisky's developing flavour is deep, slowly released and complex. This has been studied for centuries in the industry at its most detailed organic chemistry levels and it is generally reckoned that up to 70% of the final flavour and character of a whisky derives from its exposure to and interaction with the wood. Prior to the casking in the production process Douglas fir/ Oregon pine timber is used for creating the huge washback vessels that contain the wort and yeast at the fermentation stage.

**Wood extractives** *n.* These are the flavour congeners released from the **lignin** in the wood as the spirit penetrates deeper during maturation. With each successive cask filling the colour becomes lighter and the wood extractives available become less until a cask's maturation qualities are exhausted. On average a cask may be used up to three or four times in its lifetime depending on how many 'maturing years' each whisky has been in the cask on each occasion.

**Woody** *adj.* A flavour descriptor term used in tastings for whiskies whose taste on the palate produces distinctive and characteristic wooden taste notes with hints of typically resin, wood shavings, wooden pencil and pine needles.

**Wooze** *v.* (Scots) To distil. To ooze.

**Worm** *n.* The copper coil leading off from the top of the pot still which channels the ethanol vapour down into the cooling water of the condensing vessel.

**Worm Tub** *n*. A simple cold water vat or tub into which the copper worm is sunk to chill the ethanol vapour. The vapour condenses as a liquid and is run off as distilled alcohol.

**Wort** *n*. Liquor produced in the mashing process by 'cooking' the milled, malted barley. Grist malt is mixed, one part grist to four parts water, and cooked using water. Beginning at the optimum sugar extracting temperature of 64.5°C inside the mashtun the rotating lauter blades mix the grist and hot water to maximise sugar dissolution. The mashing process is marked by four 'water' stages: the first water at 64.5°C, second water at 70°C, third water at 80°C and fourth water at 90°C. The first two waters create the sugar-rich wort liquor, rich in fermentable sugars such as maltose and glucose for fermentation to alcohol. Wort is left to stand for over an hour before it is drawn off, cooled and sent on to the wash-back fermentation vessels. The lower sugar content of the third and fourth sparged matter is recycled into the next mashing batch. The solids residue left on the mashtun floor is **draff**, a sweet porridge drained and pumped out for transportation and processing as cattle feed.

**Wullie-waucht** (also **Willie-waught**) *n*. (Scots) Any hearty or generous draught of strong liquor. Most famously celebrated in the final verse of Robert Burns' *'Auld Lang Syne'*:

> And there's a hand, my trusty fiere!
> And gie's a hand o' thine!
> We'll tak' a right gude wullie-waucht,
> For auld lang syne.

# X

**Xeres** *n.* Spanish liquor made from fortified wine, and the origin of the English word *'Sherry'*. Sherry is created by adding grape spirit to fermented wine and thus increasing the liquor's final alcohol content upward of 15% ABV. It is classified as Oloroso if reaching an alcohol content of at least 17%. Sherry is recognised under European protected designation of origin status. In 1933, the 'Jerez Denominación de Origen' defined that *'Sherry'* could only come from the province of Cádiz, between Jerez de la Frontera, Sanlúcar de Barrameda, and El Puerto de Santa María.

**Ximénez** *n.* The white grape variety also known as 'Pedro Ximénez' or PX. Dried under the sun, this grape produces a concentrated sweetness fortified through ageing in **solera** casking. This Spanish grape is also the source of the sherry/fortified wines whose casks are popular with many whisky distillers. Distillers are fond of used sherry casks for the **finishing** flavour they imbue to maturing spirit. Ximénez casks are sought after by whisky producers for the rich full sherry notes. Soaked into the cask's European oak wood, these transfer over time to the maturing whisky.

# Yeast

# Y

**Yeast** *n*. The key organic trigger for the alcohol production process in Scotch whisky distilling. Yeast is the living organism that feeds on the sugar-rich wort liquor, producing ethanol by-product and converting the wort into an alcoholic beer or wash with an ABV of around 7-11%.

**Yellow Label** *n*. Launched by distiller James Robertson, *'Yellow Label'* was one of the spate of brand names that came onto the market as production and consumption of blended whisky took off in the 1880s.

**Yield** *n*. The amount of finished whisky produced from each tonne of malted barley. Producers nowadays expect to gain a minimum yield of around 405 litres from every tonne of malted barley. Continuous research and development are currently predicting possible yields attainable of around 420 litres per tonne.

**Yoker** *n*. Yoker was one of Glasgow's first and oldest legal, commercial distilleries. Founded in 1770, it was owned by the Harvie family through most of its productive life until it was closed in 1927 under ownership of the Distillers Company Limited (DCL).

# Z

**Zea Mays** *n.* Maize. Corn. Traditionally, the high starch cereal crop most popular for producing Scotch grain whisky. Each maize kernel consists of around 70% starch and 10% protein. Up to the 1980s, vast quantities of relatively cheap maize were shipped from the US to Scotland. These cargoes were unloaded for distribution into the huge dockside granaries at Meadowside in Glasgow on the River Clyde and Leith on the Forth. However, the growth of Genetically Modified (GM) maize in the US and EU restrictions on its use brought that trade largely to an end. Today, Scotland's grain whisky producers source cereals mainly from the European continent.

**Zephyr** *n.* The name of the popular barley cultivar used in malting between 1950 and 1968. The Scotch Whisky industry is reckoned to process over 800,000 tonnes of barley for malting each year. Zephyr was a step change in productivity, delivering an alcohol yield of 370-380 litres of absolute alcohol per tonne of barley. However, further advancements in agricultural science since the late 1960s have superseded Zephyr with increasing yields from varietals such as *Golden Promise, Triumph, Camargue, Chariot* and the current fave rave, *Concerto*, which can produce over 430 litres of absolute alcohol per tonne of barley.

247

# ACKNOWLEDGEMENTS

To Marion for her patience and support.

To Bairds Maltings Inverness and Tomatin Distillery for providing me with access to their operational inner sanctums.

Thanks to Ben Averis for his delightfully playful and beautifully detailed artwork.

# Select Bibliography

Archibald, Malcolm. *Whisky Wars, Riots and Murder* (Black and White Books 2013)

Barnard, Alfred. *The Whisky Distilleries of the United Kingdom* (Aaron Barker Publishing 2013)

MacDowall, R.J.S. *The Whiskies of Scotland* (John Murray 1967)

Mark, Colin. *The Gaelic-English Dictionary* (Routledge 2004)

Morrice, Philip. *The Schweppes Guide to Scotch* (Alphabooks 1983)

Moss and Hume. *The Making of Scotch Whisky* (James and James Publishing 1981)

Russell, Inge (Ed.) *Whisky Technology, Production and Marketing* (Academic Press, 2003)

Warrack, Alexander. *A Scots Dialect Dictionary* (Chambers 1911)

## ONLINE RESOURCES

Scotch Whisky Association http://www.scotch-whisky.org.uk

Learn Gaelic Dictionary http:/www.learngaelic.net/dictionary/

Dictionary of the Scottish Language http://www.dsl.ac.uk/